Rustic Chic Wedding

55 Projects for Crafting Your Own Wedding Style

To Kyle, Wyatt & Avigale:
let our family bond grow
deeper with time
like the roots of an old oak tree.

Published by Running Press,
A Member of the Perseus Books Group

Books published by Running Press are available at special discounts for bulk purchases in the United States by corporations, institutions, and other organizations. For more information, please contact the Special Markets Department at the Perseus Books Group, 2300 Chestnut Street, Suite 200, Philadelphia, PA 19103, or call (800) 810-4145, ext. 5000, or e-mail special.markets@perseusbooks.com.

ISBN 978-0-7624-4883-8
Library of Congress Control Number: 2013943527
E-book ISBN 978-0-7624-5185-2

9   8   7   6   5   4   3   2   1
Digit on the right indicates the number of this printing

Cover and interior design by Corinda Cook
Edited by Kristen Green Wiewora
Typography: Alana, Sabon, Esprit, Helvetica Neue, Angelina, and American Typewriter

Running Press Book Publishers
2300 Chestnut Street
Philadelphia, PA 19103-4371

Visit us on the web!
www.runningpress.com

Table of Contents

Chapter Four—The Country Farmhouse Wedding . . . 138

Introduction

What is a rustic chic wedding? It is a romantic campfire, fireflies dancing in the warm night sky, an old barn, a tall oak tree with an engraved heart, a love story whispering in the wind. Within these pages you will find a stunning collection of designs to enrich your special day. We have constructed a new line of timeless how-to projects that feature distressed and worn details with hints of soft urban flair. From the flower girl basket to the cake stand, each design employs our signature rustic chic concept that emphasizes natural, eco-friendly, and country, with a twist of feminine vintage couture. Each creation is a piece of art, formed from old family traditions and customized to your personality, passion, and imagination! From the ring bearer pillow to the bridal bouquet, these designs will provide you with handmade keepsakes that will last a lifetime.

Our journey started unintentionally, by chance if you will, the "good old fashioned" American way! After my son was born I had a strong desire to nest and create. My husband and I began casually creating wedding decorations in my small craft room. We opened a shop on Etsy which we named BraggingBags, and to our delight our designs were well-received and orders started trickling in. As our unique rustic chic style gained in popularity, so did our orders. We soon moved the operation into our garage, then we built an art studio on our property, then we moved into a larger studio, and then we moved into an even larger one . . . all within a year! What began as a modest hobby has grown into a lifelong dream. It is with humble gratitude that I am able to be a full-time mom and designer. As a mother to two children (a son and a daughter), I find inspiration daily in their youth and my intense love for my family. It is the smell of my son's skin after playing outside in the morning mist, loving cuddles from my daughter, and sweet kisses from my husband that I pour into each and every design I create. It is my children holding hands, giggling, and looking deep into each other's eyes as if they are sharing a secret that the rest of the world must not know. It is this purest form of love that captivates me and that I try to capture and portray in my art, and I am touched to be able to give each bride and groom simple artistry to embellish the very stepping stones of their marriage on their wedding day!

Our love story is all about a country boy finding a city girl and the extraordinary bond we share. Kyle and I make an amazing artistic team; he is a fabulous craftsman, and I love painting, sewing, and designing. When we bring our skills together we are able to create beautiful artistry and unique rustic chic designs. Throughout the making of this book we took turns writing the step-by-step directions, but Kyle's main focus was on the woodworking and engraving. Together we had such a wonderful time painting, sewing, cutting, and building—we truly want you to feel the love in each project. Kyle and I are delighted to share this clever line of wedding crafts with you; we hope it brings you a bounty of inspiration!

Life Is Good When You're In Love!

Morgann Hill

CHAPTER ONE

Tools & Materials

Walking down the aisle of your local craft store can be a heady experience for a designer. Each new material and tool is so enticing, however, the basic tools always remain faithful and are generally the easiest to work with. Every artist has their list of favorite tools and materials, as do I! The tools listed in this section will help you create the projects listed in this book as well as other DIY projects you might wish to take on.

Tools

Paint Brushes

In this book I will generally refer to three different paint brushes: flat, distressing, and lettering.

Flat Brush. To give your items the most coverage use a 1-inch or smaller flat brush. Pick a size that will accommodate the item you are painting. A smaller item will require a smaller brush, and a larger item will require a larger brush.

Distressing Brush. To give your items a distressed finish, use a scruffy paint brush.

Lettering Brush. Use small round brushes to paint beautiful letters. If you want your letters to be thin and dainty use a smaller size 0 or size 2 brush. For thicker letters use a wider round brush in a size 4.

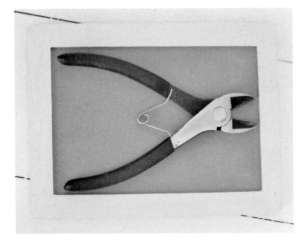

Scissors

A decent pair of general purpose scissors will work efficiently for most basic projects.

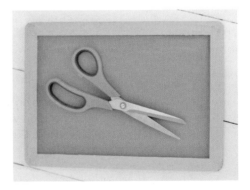

Wire Cutters

A nice pair of wire cutters is essential when working with different materials including silk flowers, rusty tin craft wire, and grapevines. Pick a pair of wire cutters that are spring-loaded and have a soft grip.

Hot Glue Guns, Super Glue, and Spray Adhesive

I prefer a glue gun that is cordless and offers a low and high temperature. Having a cordless glue gun will help you maximize your time when crafting, and dual temperatures are ideal when crafting with different materials. Gel super glue works amazingly on small projects that require a fast drying time. A multipurpose spray adhesive gives fantastic coverage. For best results, pick a general purpose spray adhesive that offers maximum hold.

Stamps & Ink Pads

I absolutely love stamps and would probably have thousands of them if I did not have self-control! Having a few different sets of alphabets, numbers, and basic shapes is sufficient to create designs that look spectacular; however, if you want to splurge you can also purchase a few ornate designs for borders and trims. Cleaning your stamps after each use will extend their usage and also keep your ink pads fresh and tidy.

Hand Drill

A basic hand drill with a few different size bits will help you drill any necessary holes to hang signs, create books, or make minor adjustments. A cordless hand drill will allow you to move effortlessly while crafting.

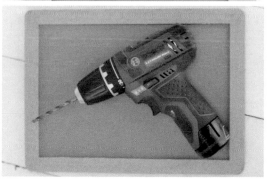

Multipurpose Wood Burner Tool/Pen

There are numerous wood burning tools on the market. The one you pick will depend on your budget and how often you plan to use it. Reading reviews will be helpful in choosing an entry level burner that suits your needs or deciding on a professional version.

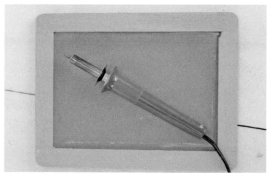

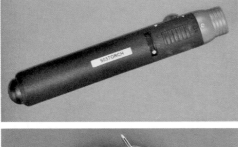

Wood Burning Torch

To create an antique finish on your designs you will need a good wood burning torch. A generous selection of torches can be found at most hardware stores and superstores. Pick a torch that will work with the level of crafting you desire to accomplish.

Chenille Needles

I like using larger chenille needles because they make hand stitching much quicker; you can maximize your crafting time creating longer stitches with thicker thread.

Sewing Machine

When I can, I try and hand-stitch most of my designs; however, sometimes you must pull out the sewing machine! A basic machine with a modest array of options is wonderful. An automatic needle threader, easy stitch selector, and adjustable sewing speed are all fantastic extra features that truly reflect the quality of your machine.

Materials

Acrylic Paint

High quality, all-purpose acrylic paint is perfect for creating small to medium size projects. Pick a paint brand that is water-based, non-toxic, and comes in a large assortment of colors. It will serve you best to pay a few extra cents for the more expensive paint, as it has better coverage and consistency.

Silk Flowers

I am always on the search for high quality, gorgeous silk flowers. Michaels and Hobby Lobby craft stores carry a large assortment of beautiful blooms and often offer great sale prices once a month. You can also find stunning silk flowers on our website, as well as Etsy and Save-On-Crafts. While I prefer to work with silk flowers, you can choose to craft with real touch flowers, paper flowers, handmade fabric blooms, or a mix.

Ribbon

Double faced satin ribbon has a gorgeous smooth texture. It is silky, shiny, and comes in a large variety of colors. When wrapping pillows and bouquets and adding trim to your projects, this ribbon will work beautifully.

Lace

I will admit that I hoard lace; when I find some that has a beautiful pattern and gorgeous lines I buy all of it and never want to use it. Lace that has an elegant design can take a basic project and completely enhance its romantic feel and quality. You can source exquisite lace at your local craft stores, flea markets, and fabric stores. You can also find bolts of lace on Etsy and Ebay.

Pearls and Rhinestones

I love to accessorize flowers and use hints of pearls and rhinestones in my shabby couture projects. Luckily, most craft stores have a large variety of pearls and rhinestones that come in an array of colors and sizes. You can pick flat-sided pearls that are self-adhesive or the traditional round pearls that you can glue or sew on. Try and pick higher quality accents that will add a touch of class and sophistication to your projects.

Felt

To create floral crowns and corsages you will need to back your flowers with felt. Simple sheets of flimsy felt work fantastic and are inexpensive and easy to trim.

Grapevine Garland

I use a ton of grapevines in my rustic projects; they are versatile and help accent amazing designs. Use thinner, more bendable garlands to create handles and lanterns, and thicker pieces for larger projects that require more of a steady hold.

Grapevine Wire

Grapevine wire is real wire wrapped in grapevines. It can be wrapped around bouquet stems, and bent to make fabulous rustic handles for baskets and lanterns.

Rusty Tin Craft Wire

A spool of 22-gauge rusty tin craft wire will help you piece together your designs and hold different elements in place. The matte brown finish blends perfectly with rustic décor.

Fabrics

I tend to use an abundance of burlap and muslin fabrics in my designs. Both of these natural materials blend nicely in many settings and offer texture that is not over the top. Burlap comes in an array of neutral colors and a few rustic patterns. Muslin is generally a blended white or cream color and comes in a variety of weights. Both fabrics are inexpensive and extremely easy to work with.

Decoupage Paste

Whenever I craft with decoupage paste I am reminded of the simplicity of kindergarten art projects—that is how easy it is to use! It comes in a wide variety of finishes (satin, flat, gloss, sparkly, antique) and is one of those elements that helps craft a project effortlessly. The clear drying paste is an all-in-one glue, sealer, and finish that bonds wood, paper, fabric, and nearly any porous surface! Mod Podge by Plaid Enterprises, has an array of beautiful finishes that work fantastic.

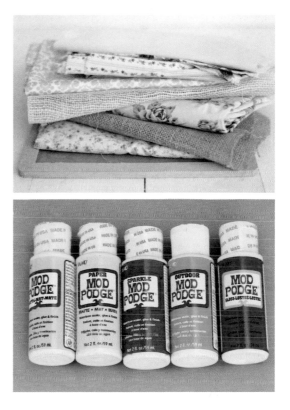

Craft Supply Stores and Websites

On our website, MorgannHillDesigns.com, you can find DIY kits and nearly all the supplies needed to create the projects in this book.

You can also find a tremendous assortment of affordable craft supplies on Save-On-Crafts.com. Traditional brick and mortar stores like Michaels, Hobby Lobby, and Joann's have nice selections of general craft supplies. Ebay.com is a good place to source antique jewelry and vintage treasures, and Etsy.com has a fabulous selection of vintage and antique finds as well as handmade supplies.

CHAPTER TWO

The Shabby Vintage Couture Wedding

If you are a lover of roses, feminine elements, and soft textures, these projects will make your heart beat fast. They combine unique vintage elements with special techniques to yield original designs. In this chapter you will learn how to quickly craft with a variety of materials, give painted items a distressed and worn appearance, and combine eclectic textures to create an eye-pleasing display. An inspiration board full of roses, vintage fabrics, rhinestones, pearls, and rustic wood will entice you to create beautiful handmade pieces for your wedding day!

Keep in mind that all of these designs can be altered and adjusted to accommodate your personal style and the colors you love. Search for fabric prints that coordinate well with your wedding colors and truly make you feel romantic and happy! Make a list of vintage treasures you want to purchase and scout out local flea markets and estate sales; you can almost always find something unique there.

Moss Guest Book Pen

A beautiful guest book is certainly deserving of a gorgeous guest book pen. By wrapping a regular ball point pen in moss-covered wire and gluing a pretty flower to the top, you can transform a plain writing utensil into something amazing! DIY weddings are all about the fine little details, and this pen is one of them.

Supply List

Ball point pen

Hot glue gun

Moss-covered wire

Wire cutters

Silk flower head

Special Note: Reuse this pen after the wedding; place it on your desk at home and let it bring you a little bit of cheer all year round.

STEP ONE: Create a ring of hot glue around the top of your pen.

STEP TWO: Tightly wrap your moss-covered wire around the pen.

STEP THREE: When the pen is completely covered, snip the wire with the wire cutters.

STEP FOUR: Add a dot of hot glue at the pen tip and secure the moss-covered wire.

STEP FIVE: Glue your silk flower to the top of the pen and hold it in place until the glue is completely dry.

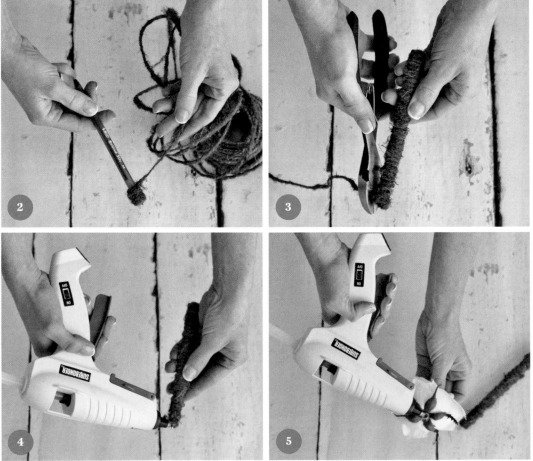

THE SHABBY VINTAGE COUTURE WEDDING

Bridal Sash

A bridal sash is a fabulous and inexpensive way to dress up the most modest of gowns. With just a few supplies needed, a plain wedding dress can be transformed into an amazing ensemble with a gorgeous focal point. Sashes aren't just for the wedding dress: bridesmaids' dresses can also be enhanced with beautiful sashes. We used white ribbon for our sash; however, you can use any color you'd like. If you have a wild side, here is your chance to show it—use a bright colored sash to add some vibrancy to your dress!

Supply List

Measuring tape

Scissors

Double faced satin ribbon (1½ or 2 inches wide, depending on your waist size and dress)

Wire cutters

Silk flowers in various sizes

9 x 12-inch sheet of felt

Hot glue gun

Pearl and rhinestone accents

STEP ONE: With your wedding dress on, measure your waist at the place where you'd like the sash to sit. Add about one or two more feet to this length so you have plenty of ribbon to tie into a bow. Cut your ribbon to the desired sash length.

STEP TWO: Using the wire cutters, cut the stems off of your silk flowers so they have nice flush backs.

STEP THREE: Cut your sheet of felt into circles large enough to cover the backs of each flower, and glue a round felt circle to the back of each flower.

STEP FOUR: Arrange your flowers on your sash until you are pleased with the layout. Usually the flowers are placed to the side, not directly in the middle; keep this in mind when you are arranging the flowers so you have more ribbon on one side to tie into a bow.

STEP FIVE: Add a dab of glue to the back of each flower and glue them into place.

STEP SIX: Add rhinestone and pearl accents to just a few of the flower blooms for some extra sparkle and glimmer!

RUSTIC CHIC WEDDING

Special Note: Don't store away your beautiful sash; wear it with your favorite pair of blue jeans and a white tank top after the wedding. Add a pair of cute wedges and you've got the perfect date night outfit!

Flower Girl Basket

With all the elements that a garden in bloom brings—budding ranunculus, twigs for the handle, and moss for the base—this darling flower girl basket is simply perfect for a shabby couture wedding. Your flower girl will feel extra-special holding such a uniquely crafted basket that you just made for her!

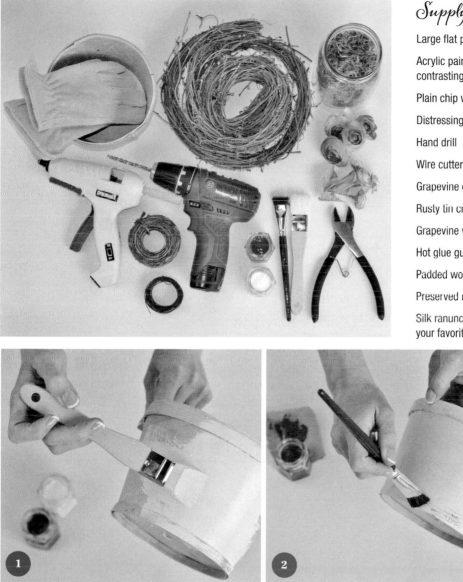

Supply List

Large flat paint brush

Acrylic paint (in two contrasting colors)

Plain chip wood container

Distressing brush

Hand drill

Wire cutters

Grapevine garland

Rusty tin craft wire

Grapevine wire

Hot glue gun

Padded work gloves

Preserved moss

Silk ranunculus (or your favorite silk flower)

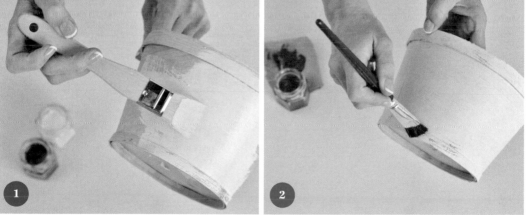

STEP ONE: Using the flat brush and one of the acrylic colors, paint the chip wood container inside and out with a light coat of paint. No need for several coats of paint, just one quickly brushed-on coat is fine.

STEP TWO: Using your distressing brush, lightly go over the edges with your contrasting acrylic paint color, giving the container a worn appearance.

STEP THREE: Drill holes on both sides of the container directly across from one another.

STEP FOUR: Cut twenty grapevine garland pieces that measure about 12 inches long. Bundle these pieces together and tie them every 4 inches with small pieces of rusty wire. This is going to be used as your basket handle.

STEP FIVE: Cut two 5-inch pieces of grapevine wire and run one through each hole on either side of the container. Arrange the handle so it fits nicely on both sides, and tie it into place using the wire pieces.

STEP SIX: Spread a thin layer of hot glue inside the container base. Cover the glue with the preserved moss. Be very careful when you spread the moss out as the glue will be very hot; use the padded work gloves to ensure you do not burn your hands while you are pressing the moss into place. When a nice thick layer is established, continue by adding a layer of hot glue along the outside rim of the basket and layering it with moss.

STEP SEVEN: On each side of the basket handle, glue into place two budding flowers. Add a few accent flowers to each side as well to add height and extra color.

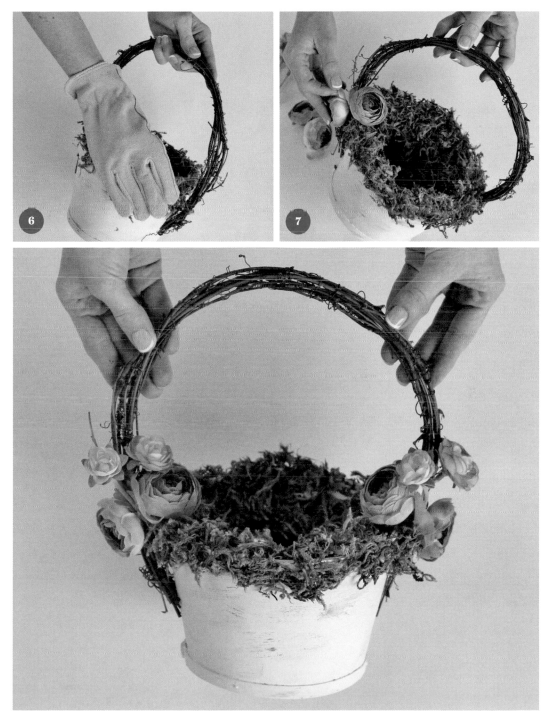

THE SHABBY VINTAGE COUTURE WEDDING

Ring Bearer Pillow

This rustic chic ring pillow is full of country charm! The natural burlap, soft satin ribbon, and silk flowers create a look that is beautiful and timeless. While we chose a palette of spring colors in pink and white, you can certainly pick colors that work well for your wedding. For example, if your wedding is in the fall, this pillow can be adorned with orange and mocha blooms. If your wedding is in the summer you might want to consider bright jewel tones. Burlap comes in many different shades, from bleached white to dark chocolate; pick one that complements your wedding colors.

RUSTIC CHIC WEDDING

Supply List

1 yard burlap fabric

Cotton six-strand embroidery floss in cream

Chenille needle

Pillow stuffing

Double faced satin ribbon

Scissors

Hot glue gun

Assortment of silk flowers to embellish pillow

Sheer ribbon

STEP ONE: Cut two 8 x 14-inch pieces of burlap. Thread your needle with the cream floss.

STEP TWO: Place your two pieces of burlap on top of each other. Begin sewing with large straight stitches, leaving a 1½-inch edge. Leave a 3 inch opening to allow for stuffing.

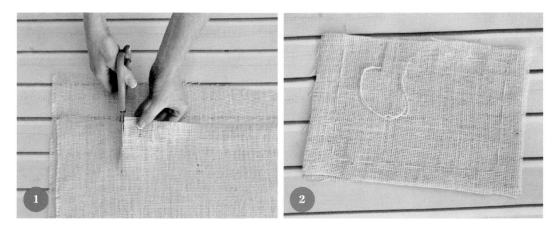

STEP THREE: Add stuffing to the inside of the pillow. Smooth the stuffing so that it is evenly dispersed inside the pillow.

STEP FOUR: Sew the remaining area of the pillow so it is now complete. Trim the edges of the pillow so they look balanced.

STEP FIVE: Cut two pieces of satin ribbon so that they fit horizontally and vertically around the pillow. Glue them into place, making all seams meet in the middle of the pillow.

STEP SIX: Glue your largest flower in the middle of the pillow. Then add the smaller flowers along the ribbon.

STEP SEVEN: Place the sheer ribbon under the satin ribbon and tie it into a bow. This sheer ribbon will be used to fasten the rings to the pillow.

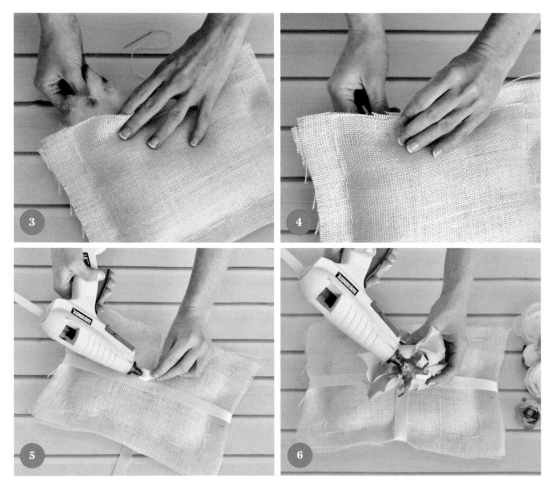

One of the easiest projects to create, these vow plaques will be cherished keepsakes. Display them during your ceremony and use them to read your vows; they'll look gorgeous in your wedding photos.

Vow Plaques

Supply List

Two 10 x 7½-inch pieces of plywood

Sponge brush

Decoupage paste

Scissors

"Bride and Groom" layout photocopied on decorative paper (page 265)

Vows printed on decorative paper

STEP ONE: Cut any trim on the paper that you do not want showing on your plaques.

Special Note: Re-purpose these vow plaques by placing them on your bedside nightstands as fun little jewelry valets.

STEP TWO: Using your sponge brush, apply a generous layer of decoupage paste to one side of one of the plywood boards. Immediately position the "Bride" layout on top and run your hands over the paper to smooth out any wrinkles.

STEP THREE: Add an additional layer of decoupage paste over the paper; be certain to seal all edges.

STEP FOUR: Allow the decoupage to dry until it is no longer sticky to the touch. Apply the vows on the opposite side. Repeat all of the steps to create the "Groom" plaque as well.

RUSTIC CHIC WEDDING

Groom

Bride

I promise to encourage your compassion,
Because that is what makes
you unique and wonderful.
I promise to nurture your dreams,
Because through them your soul shines.
I promise to help shoulder our challenges,
For there is nothing we cannot face
if we stand together.
I promise to be your partner in all things,
Not possessing you, but working with you as a
part of the whole.
Lastly, I promise to you perfect
love and perfect trust,
For one lifetime with you could never be enough.
This is my sacred vow to you,
my equal in all things

Some say I can fly on the wind, yet I have no wings.
Some have found me floating on the open sea, yet I cannot swim.
Some have felt my warmth on cold nights, yet I have no flame.
And though you cannot see me, I lay between two lovers at the hearth of fireplaces.
I am the twinkle in your child's eyes. I am hidden in the lines of your mother's face.
I am your father's shield as he guards your home.
Some say I am stronger than steel, yet I am as fragile as a tear.
Some have never searched for me, yet I am around them always.
Some say I die with love, yet I am endless.
And though you cannot hear me, I dance on the laughter of children.
I am woven into the whispers of passion. I am in the blessings of grandmothers.
I embrace the cries of newborn babies.
Others say I am a flower, yet I am also the seed.
Some have little faith in me, yet I will always believe in them.
Some say I cannot cure the ill, yet I nourish the soul.
And though you cannot touch me, I am the gentle hand of the kind.
I am the fingertips that caress your cheek at night.
I am the hug of a child.
I am Love.

Upcycled Jewelry for Your Bridesmaids

I absolutely love flea market shopping; you can find some amazing deals. I am always on the lookout for earrings or shoe clips that are missing their match. Many dealers think unpaired jewelry is useless, but these odd pieces can easily be upcyled into beautiful new creations. With a handful of old mismatched jewelry you will be able to create stunning pieces for yourself and your bridesmaids.

Supply List

Jewelry cleaner (not shown)

Collection of vintage jewelry (old earrings, shoe clips, and brooches work best)

Wire cutters or jewelry cutters

Sanding block (heavy & medium grit)

All-purpose gel super glue (make sure it works on metal)

Flat pad ring blanks (adjustable)

Glue-on pendant bails

Sheer ribbon

STEP ONE: Carefully clean each piece of jewelry. You will be amazed at what a little cleaning can do to brighten up dull old rhinestones!

STEP TWO: Using your wire cutters, nip away any back pieces, including earring posts, brooch pins, or clips. Sand any rough areas with your sanding block until the edges are no longer sharp.

STEP THREE: Lay out each piece and decide if you will use it as a ring or a pendant. Larger pieces are best for pendants, while smaller designs make super cute rings.

STEP FOUR: To create a ring, place a small dot of super glue on the ring pad. Glue the jewelry piece onto the ring pad. Hold tight for several seconds until the glue has dried.

STEP FIVE: To create a pendant, place a small dot of glue on the bail. Glue the jewelry piece onto the bail. Hold tight for several seconds until the glue has dried. Cut a piece of ribbon about 14 to 16 inches long. String the ribbon through the top of the bail to make a necklace.

THE SHABBY VINTAGE COUTURE WEDDING

Rag Balls

These colorful rag balls make the most delightful decorations for a wedding ceremony! Instead of fresh flowers that can be costly, hang these rag balls from shepherd's hooks lining the wedding aisle; they will bring texture, color, and balance to an open area.

Supply List

Scissors

4 yards assorted fabric

Hot glue gun

Twelve 6-inch styrofoam balls

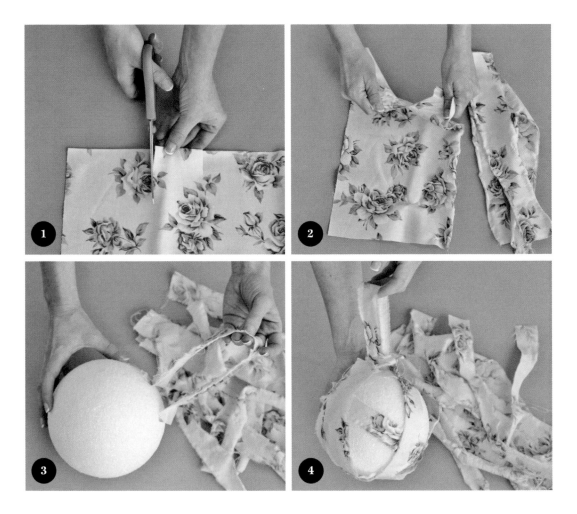

STEP ONE: Cut your fabric into 16-inch squares. Using your scissors cut a small slit at each end. Rip the fabric so it has a torn finish on all four sides. Make several small slits about 1 inch apart at the top of the fabric squares.

STEP TWO: Rip the cut slits into long pieces.

STEP THREE: Using one of the strips of ripped fabric, make it into a loop with the print facing outwards. Glue into place. This will be the handle for your rag ball.

STEP FOUR: Place a dot of glue on the back side of one of your strips of ripped fabric and glue it onto the Styrofoam ball. Wrap the fabric around the ball and glue the other end onto the ball. Continue these steps until the Styrofoam ball is completely covered.

Special Note: Save these little rag balls and use them throughout the year as decorations for parties and get-togethers. String rope through the handles and make a cute garland to hang above a buffet or dessert table.

Ceremony Backdrop

This charming ceremony backdrop is so cute. *Created from an array of vintage-inspired fabric and a large personalized wood heart, it will serve as sweet décor as you say your "I Dos." Create your rug balls (page 43) and this ceremony backdrop using the same fabrics. These two projects match beautifully and will provide a romantic DIY ceremony site.*

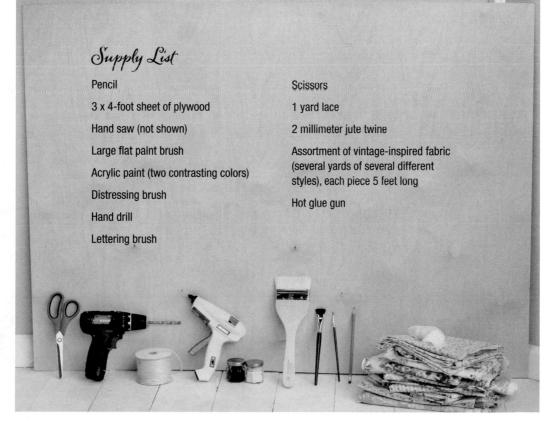

Supply List

Pencil

3 x 4-foot sheet of plywood

Hand saw (not shown)

Large flat paint brush

Acrylic paint (two contrasting colors)

Distressing brush

Hand drill

Lettering brush

Scissors

1 yard lace

2 millimeter jute twine

Assortment of vintage-inspired fabric (several yards of several different styles), each piece 5 feet long

Hot glue gun

STEP ONE: Trace a large 3-foot wide heart on your piece of plywood and cut it out using your hand saw.

STEP TWO: With the flat brush and one of the acrylic colors, paint the heart using long strokes. With the distressing brush lightly go over the edges of the heart with the contrasting color.

STEP THREE: Pencil your initials onto the heart. Drill a hole on both sides of your heart.

STEP FOUR: Go over the pencil marks with your round lettering brush and the contrasting acrylic paint color.

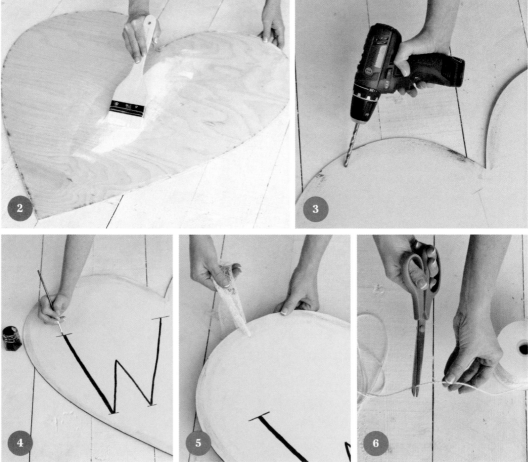

STEP FIVE: String your lace through the holes at the top of the heart.

STEP SIX: Cut a piece of twine 7 feet long.

STEP SEVEN: Cut slits in the top of your fabric and rip strips 1 inch wide by 5 feet long.

STEP EIGHT: Glue your strips of fabric around the twine, leaving 2 feet of twine on both sides.

STEP NINE: Using the lace, attach the heart to the main garland with the fabric.

Special Note: Repurpose this backdrop and use it as a unique headboard in your new love nest!

Mothers' Corsages

Surprise the moms *with beautiful wrist corsages that will make them feel extra-special on your wedding day. These gorgeous corsages, handcrafted by you, will be keepsakes they will cherish forever.*

Supply List

Scissors

Double faced satin ribbon

9 x 12-inch sheet of felt (in the same color as your ribbon)

2 silk roses

2 sprigs wax flowers

3 silk leaves

Hot glue gun

STEP ONE: Cut a 16-inch piece of ribbon.

STEP TWO: Cut your felt into circles large enough to cover the backs of your roses and the tips of your leaves, and glue them into place.

STEP THREE: Arrange three leaves on the center of your ribbon and glue them down.

STEP FOUR: Place your roses on top of your leaves with the blooms facing outward, and glue them into place. Glue your wax flowers in the middle of the two roses. Trim the ends of the ribbon in a pretty cut design.

THE SHABBY VINTAGE COUTURE WEDDING

Garden Table Numbers

Creating unique table numbers *is a brilliant way to add personality, character, and color to your reception tables. For these beautiful garden-inspired table numbers we picked a charming sand color that blended nicely with our burlap-wrapped mason jars and matching table runner. We selected pale pink paper roses which also enhanced our garden theme and matched perfectly with our fresh-picked roses.*

Supply List

Cedar wood cut into 6 x 5-inch pieces (cut the quantity you will need for your table numbers)

Medium flat paint brush

Acrylic paint (two contrasting colors)

Distressing brush

Black marker

Hot glue gun

Wire Cutters (not shown)

Paper flowers

STEP ONE: Dust off your wood pieces with your flat paint brush to ensure they are free of sawdust.

STEP TWO: Apply your base color to each cut of wood with the flat paint brush.

STEP THREE: Lightly dab your distressing brush into the contrasting color paint. Remove any access paint from the brush by dabbing it onto a paper towel, and lightly go over all the edges of the wood pieces, giving them a lovely distressed finish.

STEP FOUR: Using a marker, write out your table numbers.

STEP FIVE: Remove the stems from your paper flowers with wire cutters. Using your glue gun, make short 1-inch strands of glue along your written number. While the glue is still hot, arrange your flowers. Be careful not to make your glue strands too long, or the glue will dry before you have time to set your flowers in place.

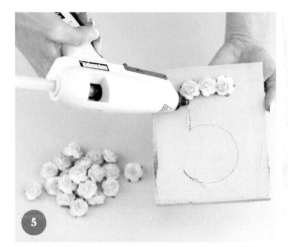

5

Special Note: These table numbers can be used well after the wedding—repurpose them as photo props to document your anniversaries, pregnancy months, or baby's birthdays.

Glitter Photo Prop Frames

Supply List

Frames (8 x 10-inch and larger)

Acrylic paint

Flat paint brush

Decoupage paste

Assortment of glitter

Mixing bowls

Sponge brushes

Decoupage spray sealer

Everyone loves a photo booth,
*and these sparkly frames are a fabulous way
to give boring props a mini makeover.*

STEP ONE: If your frames have glass, remove the glass and backs.

STEP TWO: Paint your frames to match your wedding colors and allow them to dry.

STEP THREE: Pour some decoupage paste into a mixing bowl and add a good amount of glitter. Mix together until the paste is thick and glittery.

STEP FOUR: Using your sponge brushes, paint the decoupage mixture onto your frames and carefully smooth out any clumps. Allow your frames to dry.

STEP FIVE: When your frames are completely dry, spray them with the sealer.

Special Note: If your frames come with glass, keep it; after the wedding, print your favorite photos and place them inside the frames.

Monogrammed Cake Stand

A gorgeous cake is certainly deserving of a beautiful cake stand, and this monogrammed stand is easy to make. With just a few coats of paint and some lace and pearl accents, a simple wood base can be spiffed up and transformed into a stunning personalized show-stopper.

Supply List

Simple wood cake stand base (sized to accommodate your cake)

Large flat paint brush

Acrylic paint (two contrasting colors)

Distressing brush

Lace trim

Hot glue gun

Pencil

Self-adhesive pearls or rhinestones (whichever you prefer)

STEP ONE: Using the flat brush and one of the paint colors, paint your cake stand with a solid coat of acrylic paint. Using the distressing brush and the contrasting paint color, lightly distress the edges of the stand. Allow the paint to dry.

STEP TWO: Measure around the cake stand and cut your lace trim so it can easily wrap around all sides. Glue your lace into place.

STEP THREE: Measure the front of the cake stand. In the very center pencil your last name initial. Then pencil your first name initials on either side. Generally the woman's initial comes first and the man's initial comes last. You can also personalize the cake stand with a simple initial-plus-initial design; for example, K+A.

STEP FOUR: Carefully arrange your self-adhesive pearls or rhinestones over your penciled monogram.

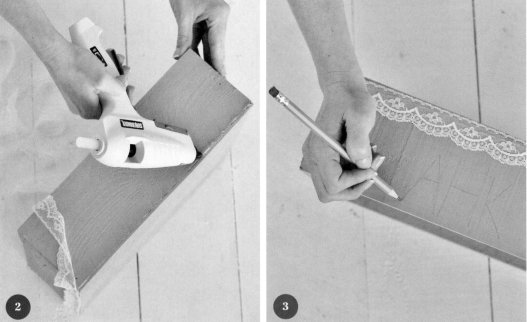

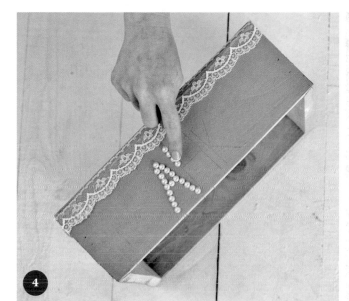

Special Note: Every year on your anniversary, pull this cake stand out of storage, splurge on a beautiful cake, and enjoy a romantic candle-light dinner with your beloved!

These upcycled treat jars are stunning! Each jar can be filled with your favorite candy, hot chocolate mix, honey—just about anything sweet! Your guests will love picking their favorite jar to take home.

Guest Favor Jars

Supply List

Baby food jars or small mason jars with lids (cleaned, labels removed)

Small flat paint brush

Acrylic paint (two contrasting colors)

Distressing brush

Acrylic sealant spray

Burlap fabric

Lace

Hot glue gun

Vintage jewelry (brooches, earrings, clips, buttons)

Something sweet to fill jars with (candy, hot chocolate mix, honey)

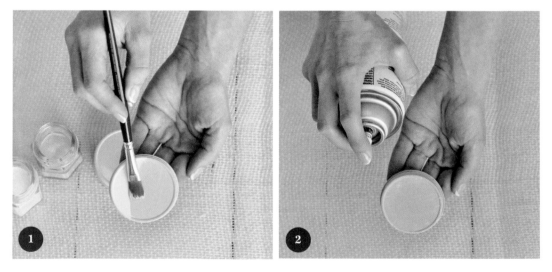

STEP ONE: Using the flat brush and one of the paint colors, paint each of your baby food jar lids with several coats of paint and allow them to dry. Using the contrasting paint color and the distressing brush, lightly distress the edges of each lid.

STEP TWO: Spray each lid with acrylic sealant spray; this will ensure that the paint does not scratch off.

STEP THREE: Cut the burlap and lace into strips wide enough and long enough to wrap around the jars. Using the hot glue gun, glue the strips of burlap around each jar and then glue the lace on top of the burlap.

STEP FOUR: Add a vintage brooch to the front of each jar and then fill the jars with your sweet treats. If you are using a piece without a pin fastener, simply hot-glue it to the lace.

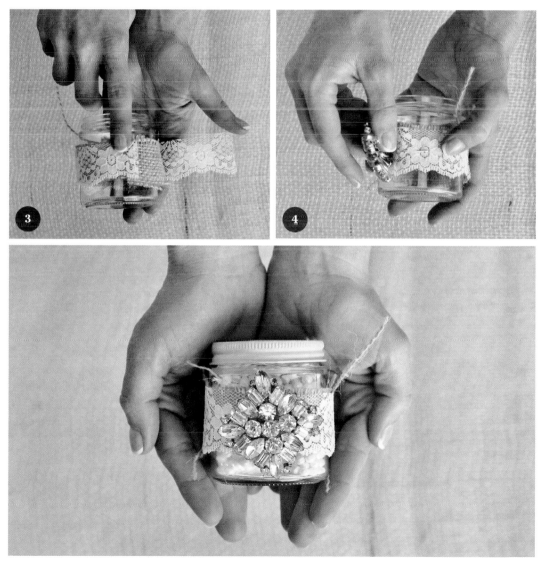

Enjoy A Late
Night Snack!

H+P

Late-Night Snack Bags

These snack bags are fabulous to offer your guests as they party the night away. Each bag can be filled with popcorn, peanuts, candy, or your special homemade trail mix. Place them in several large rustic wood crates a few hours before the final farewell, and let your guests grab a bag as they get hungry.

Supply List

Fabric

Printable fabric sheets

Sewing machine

Scissors

Popcorn, peanuts, candy, or trail mix to fill bags

Enjoy A Late Night Snack!

H+P

THE SHABBY VINTAGE COUTURE WEDDING

71

STEP ONE: For each bag, rip two pieces of fabric that measure 5 x 11 inches. Also rip one 1 x 12-inch strip. This long strip will be used to tie your bag.

Technique Tip: **Ripping the fabric instead of cutting it will give the fabric a nice worn appearance.**

STEP TWO: Using your computer, design a cute 2 x 2-inch tag to personalize your bags. Print the tag on the printable fabric sheets and rip it to size.

STEP THREE: Using your sewing machine, sew the tag to the middle of one of the larger pieces of ripped fabric, leaving a nice torn border.

STEP FOUR: Lay the two larger pieces of fabric on top of each other, pattern side facing outward. Sew the two pieces together leaving the top open and a ¼-inch border on all sides.

STEP FIVE: Fill the bag with your desired snack and tie it using the long strip of ripped fabric.

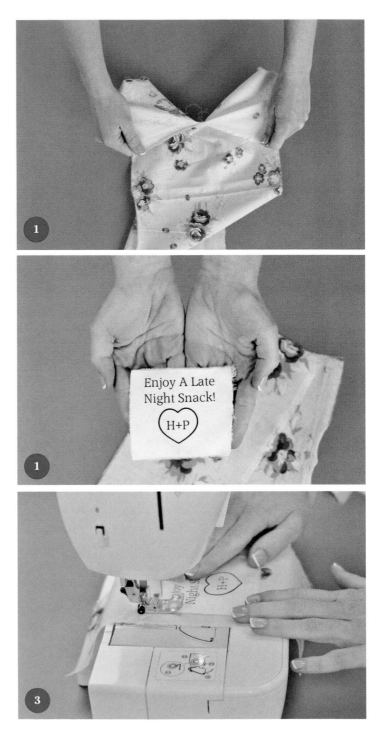

RUSTIC CHIC WEDDING

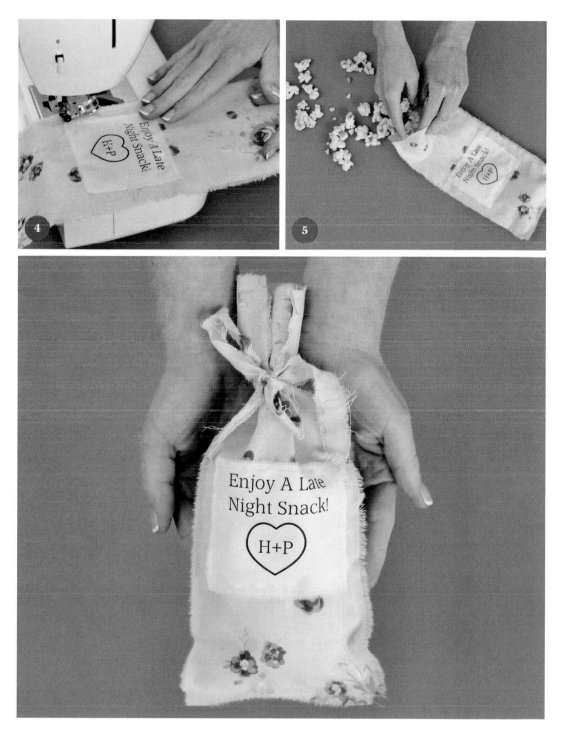

THE SHABBY VINTAGE COUTURE WEDDING

73

Unity
Candle Set

As two become one,
this unity candle symbolizes the
joining of husband and wife.

Supply List

Translucent printable vellum paper

Scissors

One pillar candle (no taller than 6 inches)

Two taper candles

Spray adhesive

Double faced satin ribbon

Hot glue gun

STEP ONE: Create the designs for your candles on the computer and print each design (the "His," "Hers," and "Ours") on separate pieces of vellum. Cut each piece of paper to size so it easily wraps around each candle.

STEP TWO: Create the pillar candle first. Spray the back of the paper with adhesive and gently guide the paper around the candle, leaving enough room at the top and bottom to add your ribbon. Smooth the paper out with your finger to release any air bubbles. Repeat these steps for your taper candles.

STEP THREE: Measure and cut your ribbon to fit around each candle. Wrap the ribbon around the top and bottom of the paper to hide the visible paper outline. Glue the ribbon into place with your glue gun, turning the edges under for a nice clean finish.

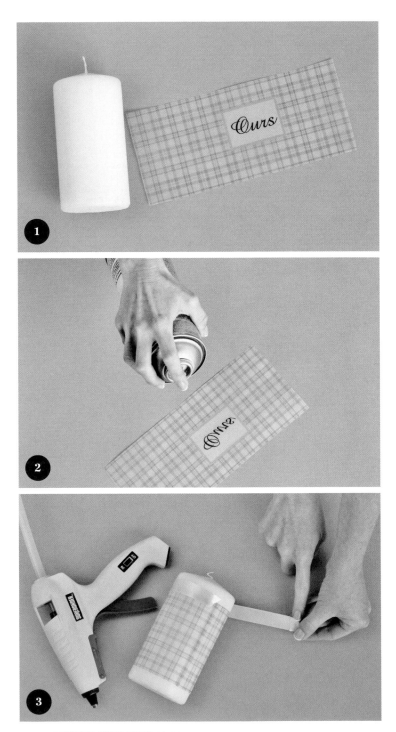

Special Note: Continue to use this candle set after the wedding. Place it on your fireplace mantle and let it remind you daily of your continued love and support of each other and the dreams you share as a couple.

THE SHABBY VINTAGE COUTURE WEDDING

CHAPTER THREE

The Rustic, Recycled & Repurposed Wedding

This chapter is all about your love story and how you wish to express it. Fun and flirty or romantic and alluring, it's your wedding and your artistry on display. With the help of recycled and repurposed materials, you will easily be able to make project after project that will create an atmosphere of love.

Many of the projects in this chapter call for vintage items that you will repurpose. Antique crocheted doilies, vintage dishes, jars with rusty lids, music sheets, and even old tin cans. Start by sending a wish list to your mother, grandmother, aunties, and siblings. Use your grandma's old doilies to create your flower girl basket and your auntie's beautiful dishes for your seating chart. Each design brings together the bond of family and highlights treasured traditions, and it's a great way to include extended family in the planning of your wedding day. However, any items your family may not have you can easily find at local thrift stores, flea markets, and garage sales.

❧

Flower Girl Crown

Every little girl loves to play dress-up, and today is *your flower girl's day to go all-out; she will feel like royalty walking down the aisle in her angelic crown. While I have chosen an array of large blooming roses and mini daisies, you can use any flowers that match your décor.*

Supply List

6 strands
grapevine garland

Wire cutters

White floral tape

Off-white felt

Silk flowers to
adorn the crown
(3 white roses,
2 pink roses,
5 bunches of
mini daisies,
4 sprigs of pink
wax flowers)

Hot glue gun

Lace

Scissors

STEP ONE: Measure the circumference of your flower girl's head and use the wire cutters to cut your grapevine garland 2 inches short of this length.

STEP TWO: Sort your grapevines so the cut pieces are free of sharp edges and all pieces are long and easily manageable. Remove any pointy and thick pieces, keeping only the thinner bendable ones. Tape the edges of the crown with floral tape.

STEP THREE: Cut your felt into round circles. Using the hot glue gun, glue these felt circles to the back of each of your flowers. These felt backings will give each flower a nice flat surface and a more workable area to glue.

STEP FOUR: Create a main focal point with your largest blooming rose and work outward from the middle. Arrange your flowers along the crown until you are pleased with their placement. Glue each rose onto the crown.

STEP FIVE: Add your daisy clusters to the top of the crown and glue them into place. On both sides of the roses glue a few wax flowers into place for balance.

STEP SIX: Complete the crown by wrapping each end in lace and securing with a dot of hot glue, leaving at least 12 inches on both sides so you can snugly tie the crown into a bow.

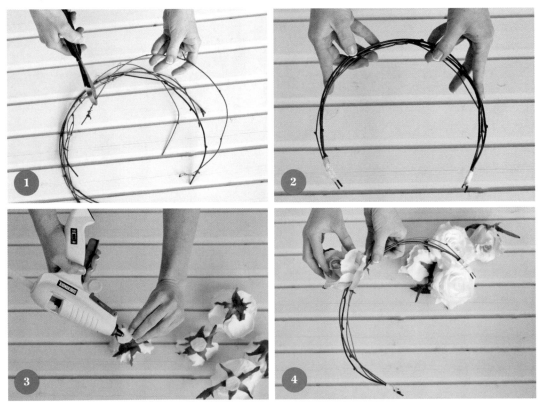

RUSTIC CHIC WEDDING

Doily Flower Girl Basket

You might know the old saying, "Something old, something new, something borrowed, and something blue." Made from an antique doily, this vintage basket will incorporate something old into your wedding plans.

RUSTIC CHIC WEDDING

Supply List

Fabric stiffener

An old tray, large enough to fit the doily

Vintage doily

Wide mouth mason jar

Jute twine

Scissors

String of craft pearls

2 rhinestone buttons

Sheer ribbon

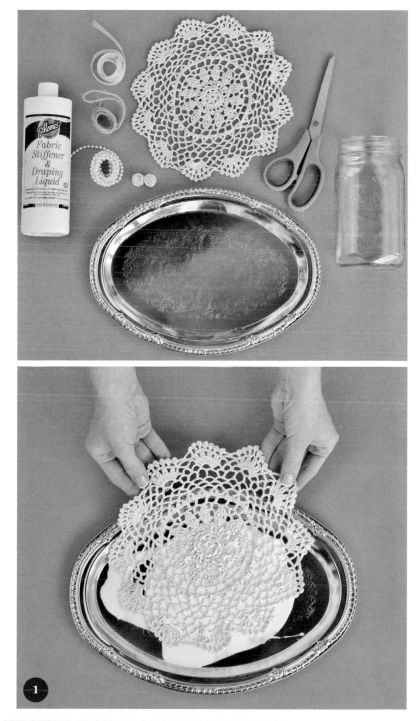

STEP ONE: Pour a thin layer of fabric stiffener onto your tray, and dip your doily in the stiffener until it is completely saturated.

STEP TWO: Place your doily on top of the wide mouth jar. Tie the sides with jute twine. Let your doily dry for at least 24 hours. The longer you allow your doily to dry the better, as you want it to take shape and be stiff.

STEP THREE: When the doily is dry and stiff to the touch, remove it from the jar. Cut the twine and allow the edges to drop into a perfectly relaxed basket. String your craft pearls through both sides of the doily to create a handle, and tie the ends.

STEP FOUR: Thread the rhinestone buttons with sheer ribbon and tie them around the pearl knots on both sides of the basket with cute little bows.

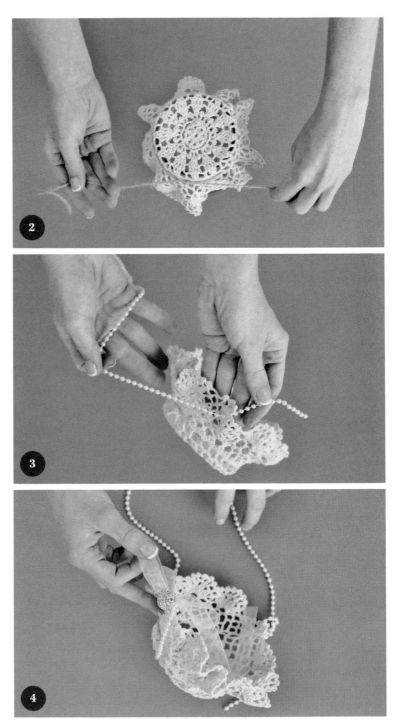

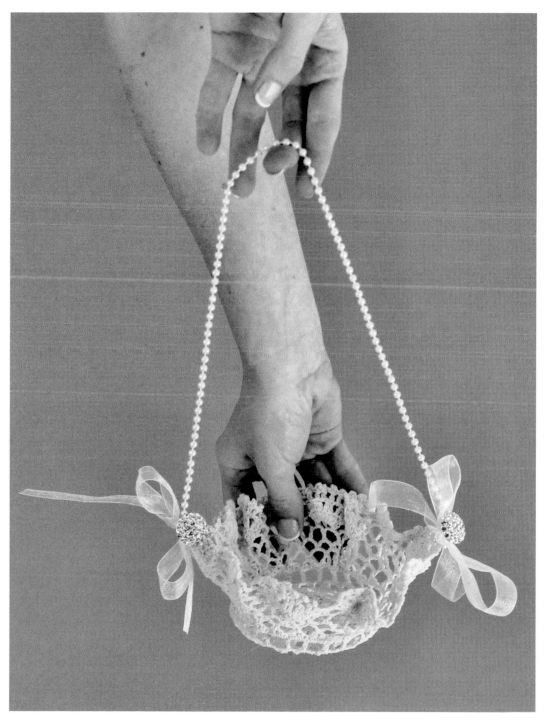

THE RUSTIC, RECYCLED & REPURPOSED WEDDING

Kissing Bell

Everyone should have a kissing bell at their wedding. *This uniquely designed bell is crafted from a few simple materials and is perfect for a rustic gathering. During your wedding reception pass the bell from table to table; when you hear the bell ring, it's time for a kiss!*

Supply List

Hand drill

Wide mouth jar
with a rusty tin lid

1 foot leather cord

Scissors

Rusty bell

Pencil

Small wood heart

Lettering brush

Brown acrylic paint

Hot glue gun

STEP ONE: Drill a small hole in the center of your rusty tin lid.

STEP TWO: Thread your leather cord through the bell handle, and then thread the open ends of the leather cord through the hole in your tin lid. Tie the cords into a tight knot thick enough that it will not slip through the drilled hole.

STEP THREE: Screw your rusty lid onto your jar.

STEP FOUR: Use your pencil to write "Kissing Bell" on your wooden heart. Go over each letter with acrylic paint using your tiny lettering brush. The letters do not have to be perfect—this is a rustic bell!

STEP FIVE: With your hot glue gun, attach the heart onto the rim of the rusty jar lid.

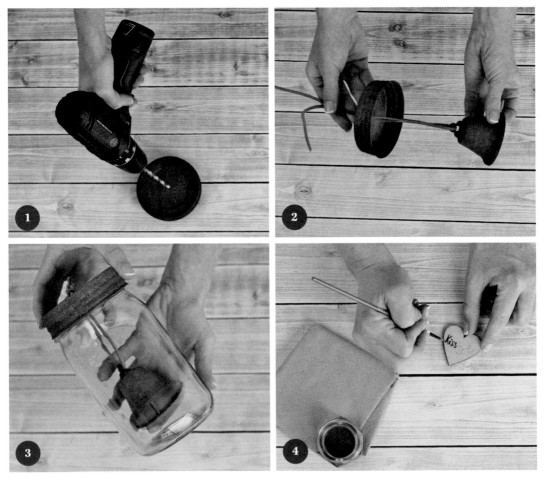

Special Note: Recycle this kissing bell in your home as a cute bookshelf or side table curio.

"Here Comes the Bride" Sign

Instead of having all of your flower girls and ring bearers carry traditional flower girl baskets and ring pillows, let them carry a special sign announcing your grand entrance. This beautiful sign has a delicate design that can be carried by one or two little ones.

Supply List

Two tall (¼ x 30-inch) wood dowels

Flat painting brush

Acrylic paint (two contrasting colors)

Distressing brush

Scissors

Burlap fabric

Hot glue gun

Paper flowers

Felt alphabet letters (at least 3 inches tall)

Lace trim

STEP ONE: Paint your wood dowels using the flat brush and one of the acrylic colors. With the contrasting acrylic color and your distressing brush, lightly antique the dowels.

STEP TWO: Cut a piece of burlap fabric 28 inches wide by 20 inches tall. Along one of the long edges of the burlap add a thin line of hot glue. Glue one of the wood dowels into place. Add another thin line of hot glue onto the dowel. Roll the burlap over the dowel. Add another thin line of glue next to the crease of the burlap and roll one more time. Repeat these steps on the other long side of the sign with your remaining dowel.

STEP THREE: Arrange your paper flowers in a swag design across the top of your sign. Place two paper flowers at the top of each dowel. Arrange your felt letters to spell out "Here Comes the Bride." Once you are satisfied with the layout and everything looks nicely balanced, glue the pieces into place with your hot glue gun.

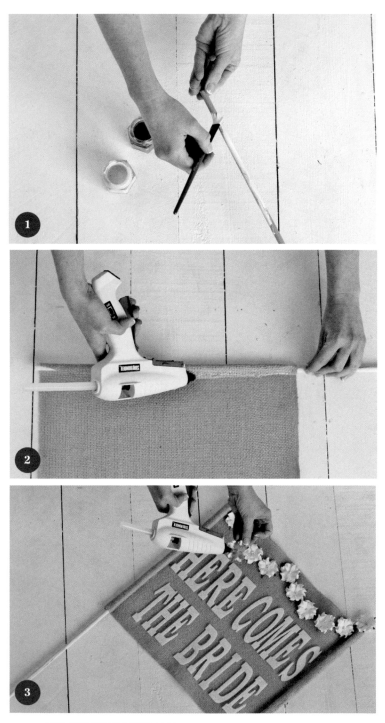

RUSTIC CHIC WEDDING

STEP FOUR: Measure the bottom of the sign and cut a piece of lace trim to fit. Glue it into place.

Vintage Plates Seating Chart

Table Three

Katie Logan

Jacob Logan

Sylvia Wise

Matt Wise

Sam Wise

Lisa Wise

Belinda Gordan

I am always on the lookout for vintage dishes I can upcycle and use as wedding décor. Stored high on the shelves in my studio, I have a gorgeous collection of old dishes with delicate floral borders, bright pink roses, and ornate designs. Vintage dishes can add a stunning touch to almost any event, and this assortment of antique plates repurposed as a unique seating chart offers your guests one of the first glimpses into your DIY wedding

Table One

Terry Fisher
Michael Fisher
Lara Thomas
Scott Thomas
Kris Ertyl
Mary Ertyl
Luke Dawson

Table Two

Stan Lewis
Alisha Lewis
Kara DeLaroche
Martin DeLaroche
Andrew Ritz
Mark Ritz
Pauline Stomk

Supply List

Collection of vintage plates that have a plain center (one per table)

Rub-on transfer paper

Scissors

STEP ONE: Wash and dry your dishes thoroughly.

STEP TWO: Measure the inside diameter of your plates. Create the seating chart design for each table on your computer, making sure each design will fit on your individual plates.

STEP THREE: Follow the printing instructions for your rub-on transfer paper, and print your table seating charts. Make sure you mirror the layout before printing! Trim the extra paper away from your design as closely as you can.

STEP FOUR: Lay each design on a plate to ensure the spacing is nice. Remove the first layer of film. Place the design back onto your plate and smooth out the paper to release any air bubbles. Rub the paper with the stick provided until the design looks faded on the paper.

STEP FIVE: Remove the film paper. Repeat these steps until you have your entire seating chart completed.

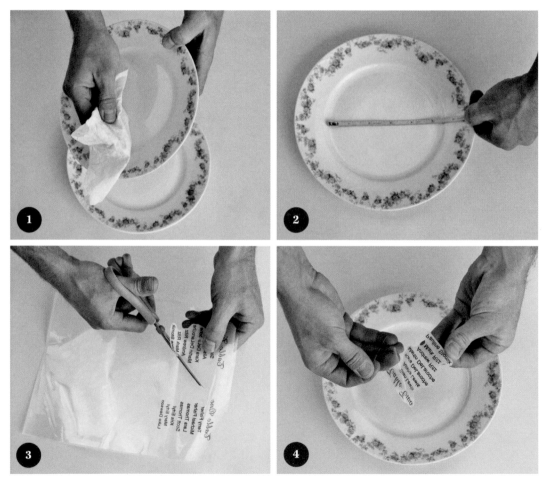

Special Note: This unique seating chart can be styled many different ways. We hung our plates from an old door; however, you can also style these on a table with the plates arranged on easels.

"Kissing Booth" Sign

This flirtatious "Kissing Booth" sign is the perfect accessory for a romantic wedding. Create a special little photo booth for your guests, and let them smooch for the camera.

Supply List

Sponge brush

One 6 x 24-inch cedar plank

Walnut wood stain

Thin, 5-inch tall wood alphabet letters

Medium flat paint brush

Acrylic paint (cream and one contrasting color)

Distressing brush

Hot glue gun

STEP ONE: Using the sponge brush, go over your cedar plank with walnut wood stain. Allow the stain to dry overnight.

STEP TWO: Using the flat brush, paint the wood alphabet letters in cream. Allow the paint to dry, and then distress the edges using the distressing brush and contrasting color.

STEP THREE: Arrange your letters on the cedar board to ensure that they fit accordingly, and then glue each letter into place with your hot glue gun.

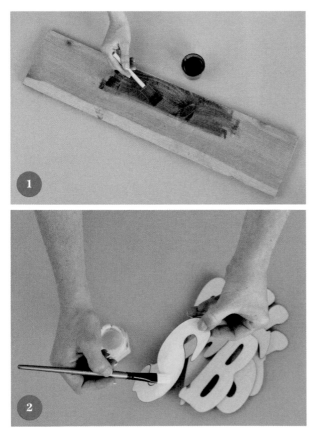

RUSTIC CHIC WEDDING

3

Special Note: After the wedding give your sign a good coat of outdoor polyurethane spray to seal the wood. You can then display the sign outdoors in your garden!

Love Notes Table Runner

With vintage sheet music and lace *you can create inexpensive table runners that will add a gorgeous touch to your reception décor. The faded paper, musical notes, and ornate lace are an eclectic mix that enhances any DIY wedding design.*

Supply List

Vintage sheet music

Lace with a straight border

Glue stick

Hot glue gun

Scissors

Special Note: Spread the love and gift these table runners to your bridal party to use in their own homes.

STEP ONE: Measure the table you are creating the table runner for. Calculate the number of sheet music pages and the length of lace you will need, making certain to add several extra inches so that the lace will overlap the sheet music on all four corners of the runner.

STEP TWO: Using a glue stick, add glue to the torn edge of one of the sheet music pages and secure the other sheet so that they overlap, covering the torn edge. Smooth the glued edge. Continue by gluing new sheets to cover the torn edges. All torn edges should overlap on the inside seam of the table runner with the clean edges as the border. Repeat these steps until the table runner is as long as you'd like it to be.

STEP THREE: Measure your lace to accommodate all four sides of your table runner, and then cut it into four separate pieces being careful to add an extra 2 inches to each cut so that the edges will overlap. Using your glue gun, apply a thin layer of glue along each edge of the table runner, and smooth your lace into place, again being very careful to include the over-hanging 2 inches of lace at each corner.

STEP FOUR: Using a pair of scissors, make a clean diagonal cut into one corner of the lace. Trim the sharp edge to make a nice scalloped edge. Add a dot of glue to the two cut corners and over-lap them. Repeat this process for all four corners to finish the lace edging.

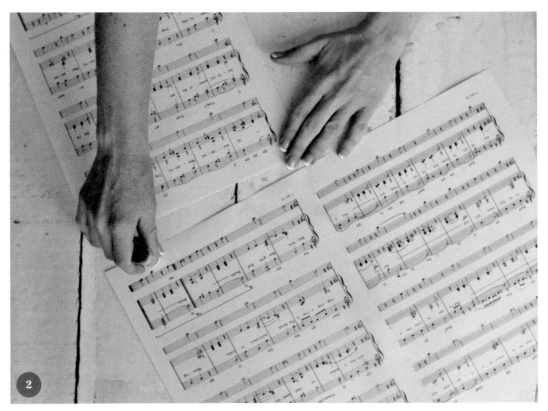

RUSTIC CHIC WEDDING

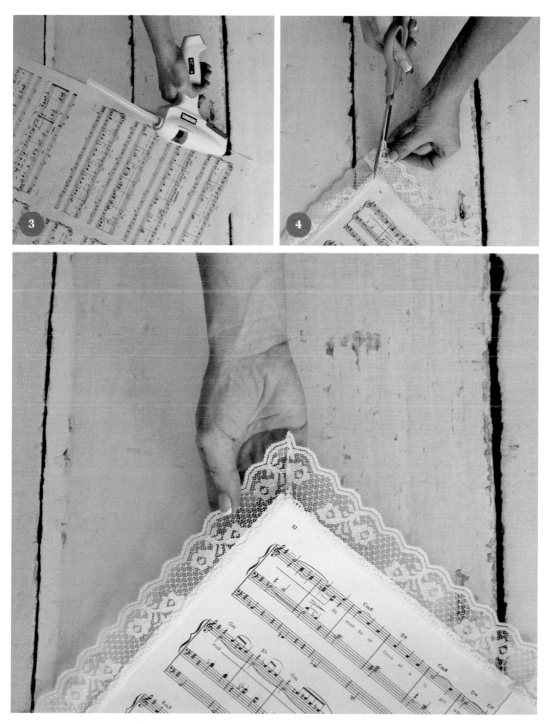

THE RUSTIC, RECYCLED & REPURPOSED WEDDING

Wedding Dress Hanger

On your wedding day you will change from "Miss" to "Mrs." As you get dressed and put on your stunning wedding dress, it will be your last time as a "Miss." When you return that evening and hang up your wedding dress, you will then be able to turn around your hanger—you are now a "Mrs."!

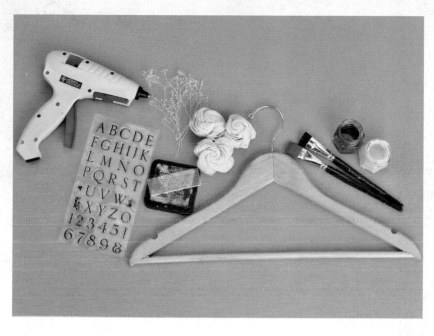

Supply List

Medium flat paint brush

Wood hanger

Acrylic paint (two contrasting colors)

Distressing brush

Clear alphabet stamps

Clear stamping block

Stamp ink

Dried baby's breath (or similar accent flower)

Hot glue gun

3 paper or silk flowers of various sizes

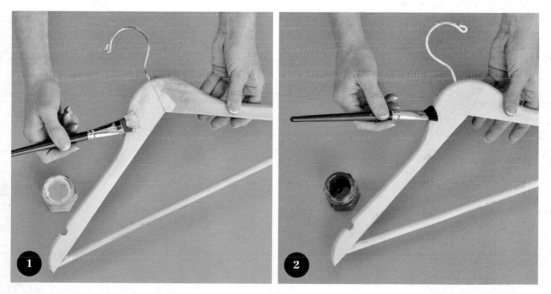

STEP ONE: Using your flat paint brush, paint the hanger with a light coat of one of the acrylic colors. Allow the paint to dry.

STEP TWO: With the distressing brush, lightly stroke the edges of the hanger with the contrasting acrylic color to give it a time-worn appearance.

STEP THREE: Arrange your clear alphabet stamps to spell out "Mrs." on your clear stamping block. Press the stamp onto your ink pad, being careful not to press too hard. Before stamping onto the hanger, turn the block over to make sure there is no extra ink on the block. If there is, wipe it away before you stamp the hanger. Once you are sure the ink is on the alphabet letters only, stamp your hanger. Repeat the above steps for "Miss" on the opposite side of the hanger.

STEP FOUR: Break off two or three little sprigs of baby's breath. Place a dot of hot glue on the stems and glue them into place on the hanger.

STEP FIVE: Place a dot of glue on the back of each paper flower. Attach the flowers so they encircle the hanger hook; position the largest flower on one side and the two remaining flowers on the opposite side.

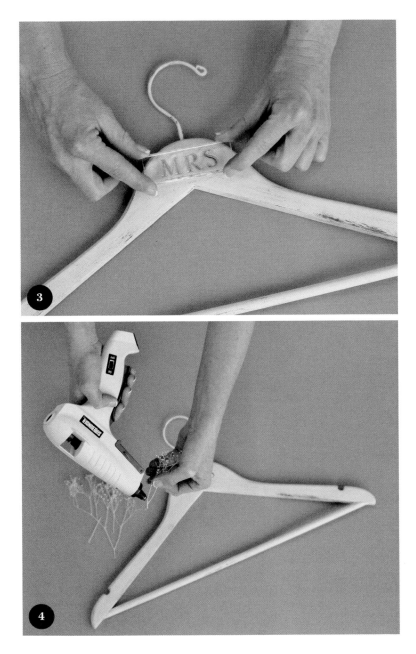

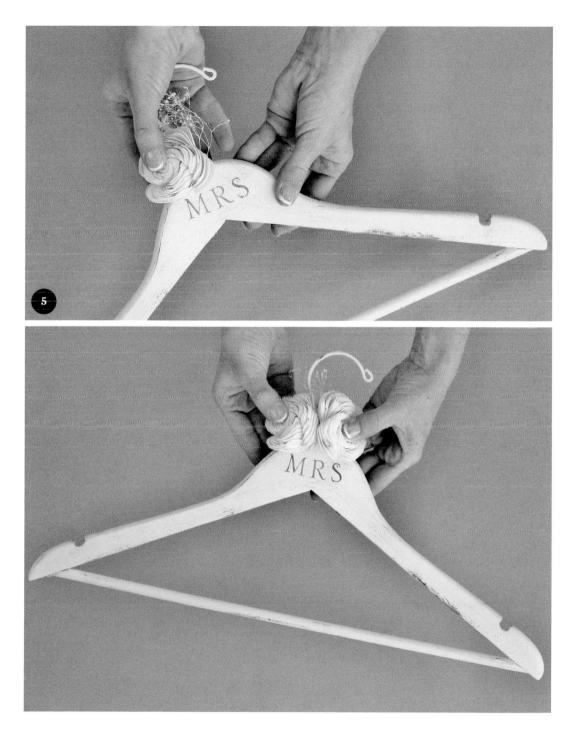

Birch Bark Cones

These rustic chic birch cones are absolutely beautiful. *They add a hint of fairytale romance to trees, gates, pews, and chairs! You can fill each cone to overflowing with wild flowers and hang them wherever a bit of color is needed.*

STEP ONE: Cut each birch bark sheet with the hobby knife to measure 9 x 11 inches.

STEP TWO: Roll the bottom corner to the center and glue it into place.

STEP THREE: Continue rolling the birch and gluing as you go. Your completed cone should have a 5-inch opening.

STEP FOUR: Use your hand drill to make holes on both sides of the cone.

STEP FIVE: Cut a piece of grapevine wire and bend it into the shape of a handle. Attach the handle through the holes on either side of the cone. Bend the ends of the grapevine to hold it in place.

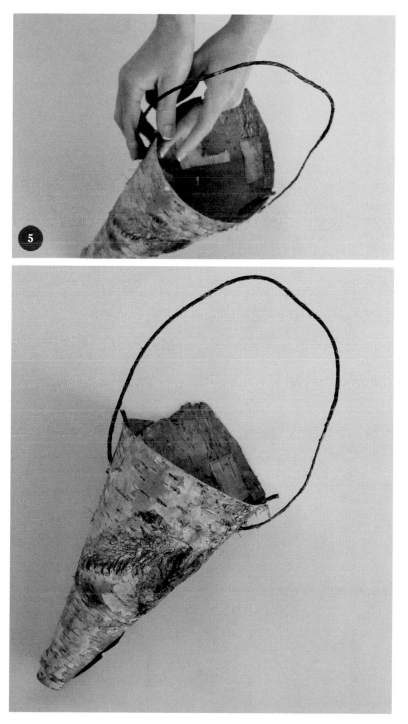

TAKE ONE
And Watch Love Grow

Tin Can Wedding Favors

These recycled-can wedding favors *are perfect for a garden, rustic, outdoor, or eco-friendly wedding. Filled with freshly cut or planted flowers, these vases are lovely gifts to offer guests as a remembrance of your wedding day.*

Supply List

Old tin cans

Various garden and love-related phrases printed on standard paper

Scissors

Sponge brush

Decoupage paste

High-gloss decoupage finish spray (optional)

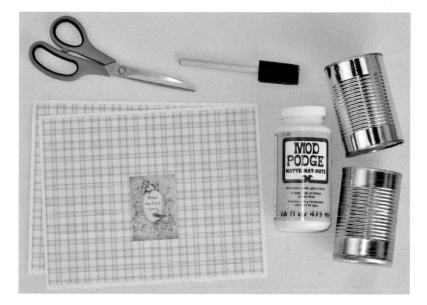

STEP ONE: Clean your cans and remove any labels. Measure the cans and cut your paper so the phrases wrap around the cans at the correct height.

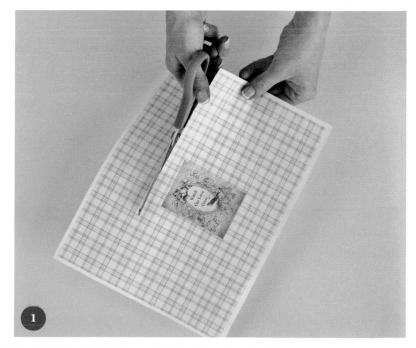

STEP TWO: Using the sponge brush, apply a thick layer of decoupage paste to each can. Position your paper and wrap it around the can. Use your finger to smooth out any air bubbles.

STEP THREE: Apply another generous layer of decoupage paste on top of the paper on each can. If desired, spray each can with high-gloss finish and allow it to dry.

STEP FOUR: Fill your cans with either cut or planted flowers.

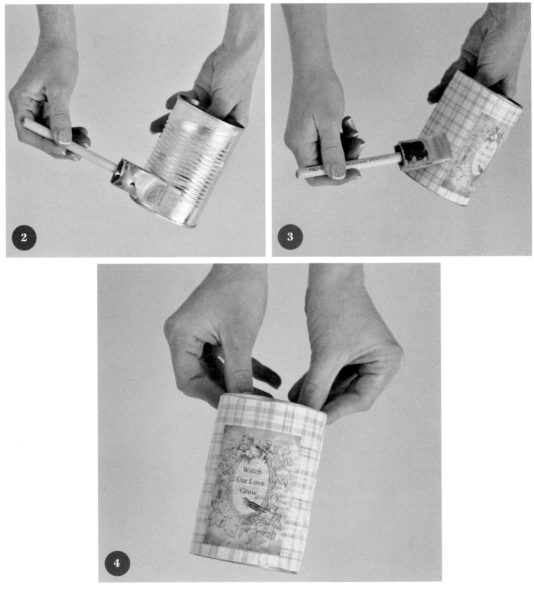

Old Frame Escort Card Holders

Old vintage frames are wonderful for repurposing into clever escort card holders your wedding guests will love! I went shopping on Ebay and found a collection of mismatched frames that had already been painted a fun and bright celery color. By adding a backing of burlap, some lace, and mini envelopes with escort card inserts, I quickly revamped these frames into wedding décor. To display the frames we hung them on an old architectural screen and added a few bud vases full of fresh flowers. This beautiful vignette is a cheerful way to welcome guests and show them to their seats.

Supply List

A collection of old frames in various sizes and shapes

Acrylic paint (for the frames)

Large flat paint brush (to paint your frames)

Distressing brush (to paint your frames)

Measuring tape

Burlap fabric (you will need enough fabric to line the inside of each frame)

1-inch-wide lace (you will need enough to make several rows in each frame)

Sewing pins

Hot glue gun

Mini envelopes

Mini escort card inserts

Pen

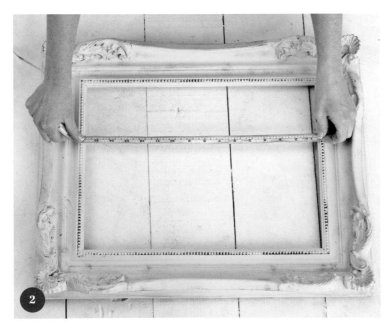

STEP ONE: Our frames were already painted; however, if you want to change the color of your frames go ahead and paint them. Start by applying a quick layer of acrylic paint with the flat brush, and then distress the edges in a contrasting color with the distressing brush. Allow the paint to dry.

STEP TWO: Take the inside measurements of each frame. Add an extra ½-inch border so you have room to glue the fabric to the back of your frame.

STEP THREE: Cut your burlap to size for each frame.

STEP FOUR: Lay your lace in rows on top of the burlap and cut the edges of the lace so they are the same width as your burlap. Place your frame on top of your arrangement to make sure the lace is straight and visible. Pin your lace into place using the sewing pins. Add a thin line of hot glue along the bottom of the lace and glue it onto the burlap, removing your pins as you glue the lace down. Make sure only the bottom of each lace row is glued down; the top will need to be open to create pockets for the escort cards. Repeat this step for all the lace rows.

STEP FIVE: When all the lace rows are glued into place, glue your burlap to the back of the frame. Make sure to pull the burlap tight as you glue it down. Allow the glue to dry.

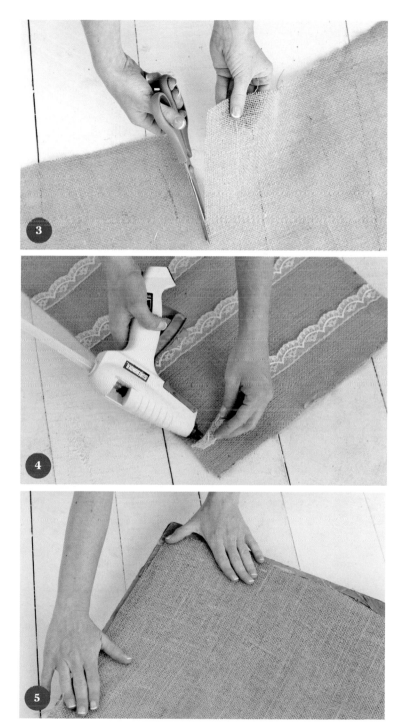

THE RUSTIC, RECYCLED & REPURPOSED WEDDING

STEP SIX: Write your guests' names on the outside flaps of the envelopes. On the inside card write their table numbers.

STEP SEVEN: Arrange your mini envelopes along the lace rows. Place a dot of glue in between each envelope so the lace is glued down in these spots. This will create pockets for the envelopes so they do not fall out. Repeat all of these steps until you have the number of frames completed to accommodate all of your escort cards.

Special Note: Give these frames to the members of your wedding party and to those who helped plan the wedding! They make darling message boards for the home office. Slip a little note or grocery list behind the lace, and these frames are transformed into useful home décor.

Chalkboard Place Cards

These beautiful place cards are easy *to create and will make your tables look so cute. They can also be used as buffet markers and table numbers by adjusting the size.*

Supply List

12 x 2-inch sheets thin balsa wood (about 1/16 inch thick)

Hobby knife

Two sponge brushes

Chalkboard paint

Decorative border stamp

Ink pad

Medium flat paint brush

Acrylic paint

Mini balsa wood blocks

STEP ONE: Cut your thin balsa wood sheets into 2 x 3-inch rectangles using your hobby knife.

STEP TWO: Using a sponge brush, paint the front of each rectangle with chalkboard paint and allow the paint to dry.

STEP THREE: Press your decorative stamp onto the ink pad and then stamp the front of each place card. Let the ink dry.

STEP FOUR: Using the flat brush, paint the opposite side of each place card with your acrylic paint. Let it dry, and then use the same paint to lightly distress the border of the chalkboard side. Allow the paint to dry.

STEP FIVE: Cut your mini balsa blocks into 1-inch chunks using your hobby knife and paint them with the acrylic paint.

STEP SIX: Using your hot glue gun, glue a balsa chunk to the acrylic-painted side of each place card.

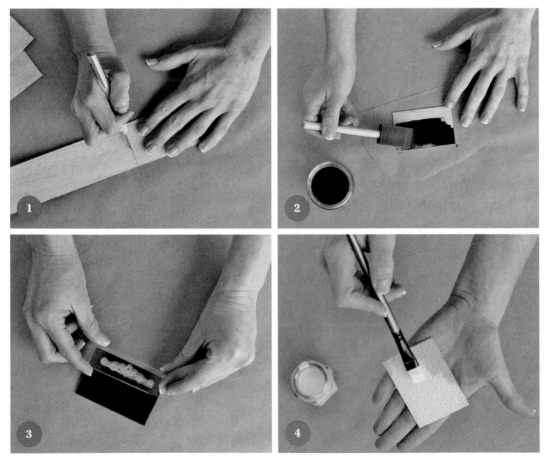

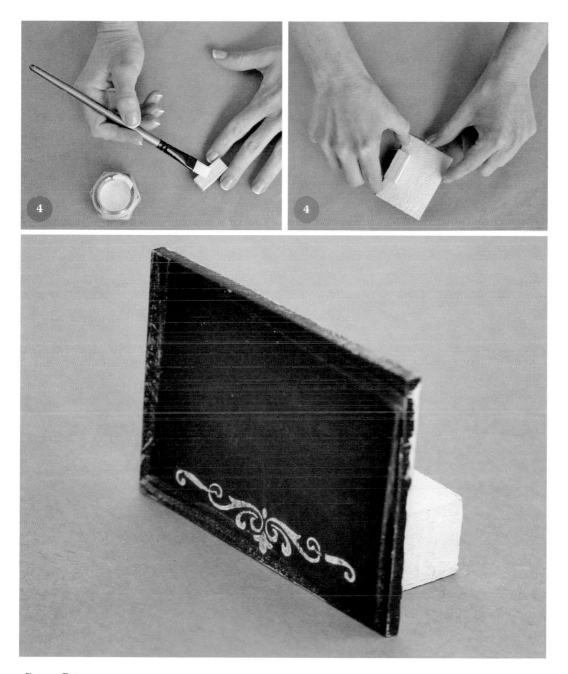

Special Note: These place cards are made with a chalkboard finish; therefore, they can be wiped clean and used time and time again. Use them for holiday parties and get-togethers as food markers, drink signs, and party signage.

Farewell Bubbles

Place these little farewell bubbles on a table near the area where you will depart as the new Mr. & Mrs. at the end of your big day. Offer a jar to each guest and let them gather outside and blow bubbles as a grand finale to a memorable night!

Supply List

Small flat paint brush

Acrylic paint (two con-trasting colors)

Glass baby food jars (cleaned thoroughly, labels removed)

Distressing brush

Acrylic sealant spray

Scissors

Burlap fabric

Hot glue gun

Wire cutters

Rusty tin craft wire

Small wood heart (to use as a guide for making your heart wands)

Twine

Bubble solution

STEP ONE: Using the flat brush and one of the acrylic paint colors, paint each of your baby food jar lids with several coats of paint and allow it to dry. Go over the edges of each lid with your distressing brush and your contrasting acrylic paint color. Allow the paint to dry.

STEP TWO: Spray each lid with acrylic sealant spray. This will ensure that the paint does not scratch off.

STEP THREE: Cut your burlap fabric into strips wide and long enough to wrap around the jars. Glue the strips of burlap around each jar with your hot glue gun.

STEP FOUR: Cut a strip of rusty wire about 16 inches long. Bend the wire around your wood heart so it takes the shape of it. Twist the extra wire together to form a stem, and trim the stem to your desired length with the wire cutters. This will be used as a wand to blow bubbles. Repeat with as much wire as necessary to make wands for all of your guests.

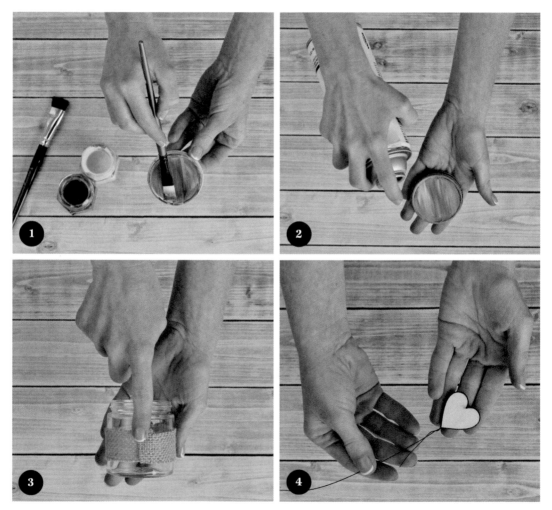

STEP FIVE: Fill your jars with bubble solution and secure the lids. Tie a piece of twine around each jar. Secure the lids on the jars and snugly position the wands into the knots of the twine.

THE RUSTIC, RECYCLED & REPURPOSED WEDDING

Every LOVE STORY is Beautiful But OURS is my Favorite

Hat Box Cake Stand

As you embark on your journey as husband and wife, this cake stand represents the many chapters you will write together. With its very simple design, this cake stand showcases the allure and romance of marriage and the story of your romantic courtship. Use it as a keepsake box after the wedding to store your special mementos.

Supply List

Old hat box

Vintage love story book or novel

Decoupage paste

Sponge brush

High-gloss decoupage finish spray (optional)

STEP ONE: Carefully tear out all of the pages from your book. Tear all the edges so they look worn and aged.

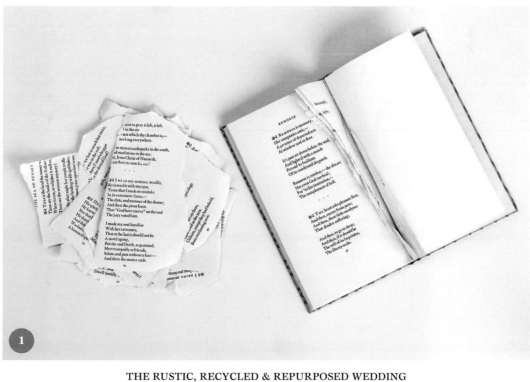

STEP TWO: Remove the lid from your hat box and put it aside. Working in small sections and using the sponge brush, add a thick layer of decoupage paste to the outside of your hat box. Arrange the pages over the paste, wrapping the edges of paper over the top and bottom edges of the box.

STEP THREE: Paint another layer of decoupage paste over the book pages to secure them into place. Repeat these steps until the entire hat box is covered. If desired, spray the box with high-gloss finish. Once the decoupage paste (and optional finish) has completely dried, replace the lid on the box.

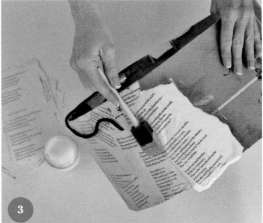

Special Note: If your wedding cake is going to be heavy you might need to fill your hat box with stacked books or magazines to allow for more weight. Discuss this with your baker prior to crafting your cake stand.

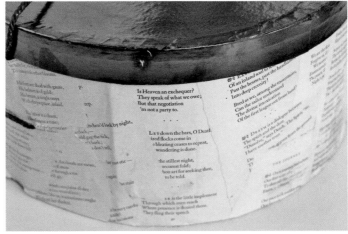

Upcycled Tray Magnet Board

Use these cute magnetic board to hold little signs around your wedding reception; they'll add a simple touch of shabby chic to the décor.

Please Sign
Our Guest Book

Supply List

Nickel-plated tray

Flat paint brush

Acrylic paint (two contrasting colors)

Distressing paint brush

Wood hearts

Hot glue gun

Magnets

STEP ONE: Using the flat brush and one of the acrylic colors, paint your tray with a quick layer of paint. Use the distressing brush and the contrasting acrylic color to add an antique finish to the tray. Allow the paint to dry.

STEP TWO: Paint and distress your wood hearts (see step one for technique).

STEP THREE: Using your glue gun, glue a magnet to the back of each heart.

Special Note: After the wedding, leave each other sweet love notes on this adorable sign!

RUSTIC CHIC WEDDING

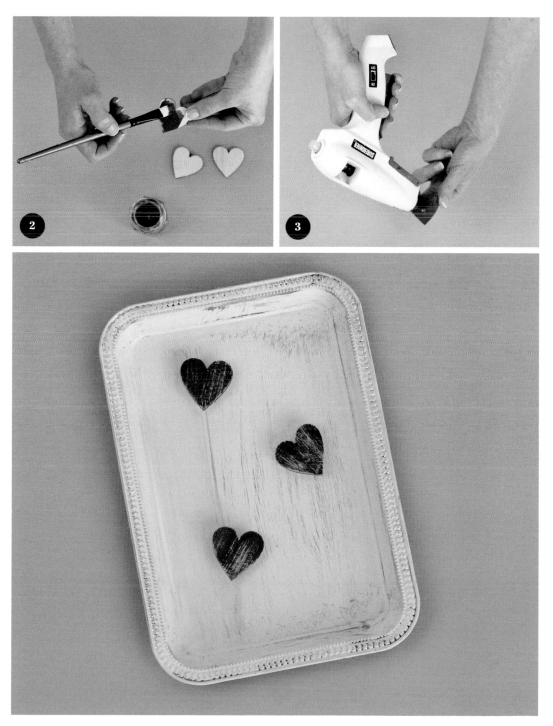

THE RUSTIC, RECYCLED & REPURPOSED WEDDING

CHAPTER FOUR

The Country Farmhouse Wedding

This chapter is all about the warmth of Southern hospitality and lovely little pieces that make a big statement! In this section you will learn how to effortlessly use a wood burning tool to hand-engrave and personalize many designs.

Using a well-balanced array of antique architectural elements and creative supplies, you can create a collection of amazing accessories for your wedding. Reclaimed materials and time-worn wood are the main ingredients in this chapter. Neutral colors and soft natural fabrics create timeless designs, and a mixture of burlap, lace, and soft muslin fabrics enhances the earthy designs and natural ambiance of a comfortable farmhouse wedding.

Bridal Crown

A gorgeous floral crown can embellish a simple dress. The natural beauty of the wedding crown brings a touch of romance and enchantment that is truly remarkable.

Supply List

Measuring tape

Wire cutters

Grapevine wire

White floral tape

Scissors

Cream or white felt

Silk flowers to adorn the crown (I used cabbage roses and mini ranunculus)

Lace trim

Hot glue gun

STEP ONE: Measure the circumference of your head. Cut two pieces of grapevine wire that measure 1 inch short of this measurement. Twist the grapevine wires together.

STEP TWO: Tape the edges of your crown with floral tape.

STEP THREE: Cut your felt into circles large enough to cover the backs of each rose. Using the hot glue gun, glue a felt circle to the back of each rose. These backings will give each flower a nice flat surface and more workable room to glue it onto the crown.

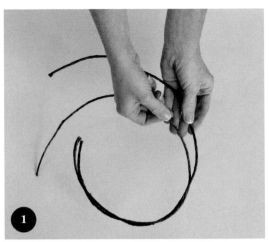

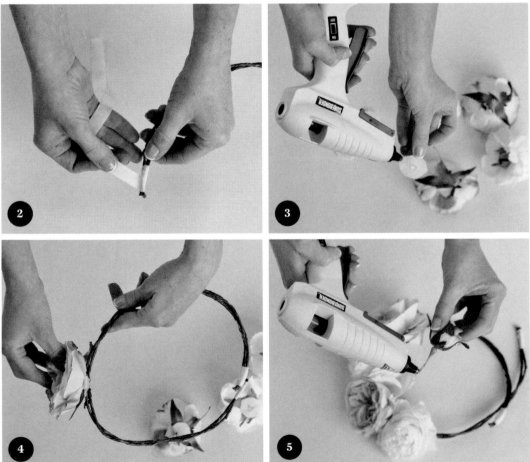

STEP FOUR: Create a main focal point with your largest rose and work outward from the middle. Arrange your flowers along the crown until you are pleased with their placement. Glue each flower onto the crown.

STEP FIVE: Add your mini ranunculus and smaller roses where there are open spots that need to be filled.

STEP SIX: Complete the crown by wrapping each end in lace trim and securing with a dot of hot glue, leaving at least 12 inches on both sides so you can tie the crown into a beautiful bow.

THE COUNTRY FARMHOUSE WEDDING

S'MORE BAR

There is something truly romantic about *a crackling fire. Bring this nostalgia to your wedding with a campfire and a s'mores dessert bar!*

S'more Sticks

Supply List

Sticks at least (24 inches long and ½ to ¾ inch in diameter)

Loppers or hand saw

Woodworking knife or sharp razor knife

S'more supplies

THE COUNTRY FARMHOUSE WEDDING

STEP ONE: Cut your sticks to the length desired using your loppers or hand saw.

STEP TWO: Using your woodworking knife, whittle a point about 3 inches long that exposes the inner core of the wood on each stick.

STEP THREE: Halfway down your point, angle your cuts toward the handle of the stick, giving the tip a diamond shape which will help hold the marshmallow.

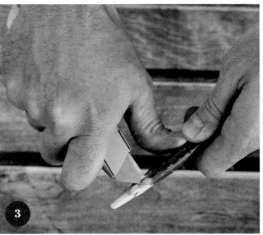

RUSTIC CHIC WEDDING

DIY S'Mores

There is something truly romantic about a crackling fire. Bring this nostalgia to your wedding with a s'mores dessert bar complete with a campfire. Place a long and narrow planter box on an old farm table and fill it with charcoal and several gel fuel cans.

Organize your handmade s'more sticks in a medium-size hay bale, sharp ends facing down. Scatter the table with tree slices and wood boxes filled with marshmallows, chocolate, graham crackers, peanut butter, and sprinkles. Your guests will love making their own delicious s'mores with all the treats you offer.

Farmhouse Menus

Let your guests know *what's for supper with these naturally inspired menus. Place one at each place setting or one at each table; they double as primitive décor.*

Supply List

5 x 7-inch birch wood plaques

Sponge brush

Light walnut wood stain

Printable fabric sheets

Burlap fabric

Hot glue gun

Antique metal fasteners (copper finish)

Scissors

Hand drill

Pencil

STEP ONE: Stain your wood plaque using the sponge brush and the walnut stain. Allow the wood to dry.

STEP TWO: Design your dinner menu so that it measures 3½ x 5½ inches, and print it on your printable fabric sheet following the manufacturer's instructions. Rip the edges of your menu sign so the outline is worn and aged looking.

STEP THREE: Cut a piece of burlap fabric that measures 4 x 6 inches.

STEP FOUR: Using your hot glue gun, glue the menu sign to your piece of burlap.

STEP FIVE: Arrange the burlap on top of your piece of wood. Make pencil marks in the four corners of the burlap. Drill holes where the pencil marks are.

STEP FIVE: Place your metal fasteners in the drilled holes.

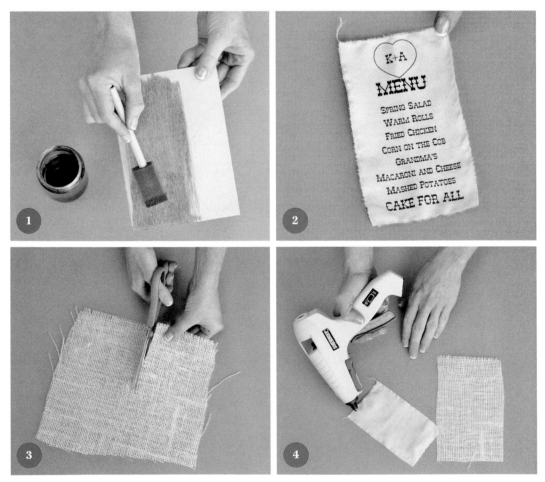

THE COUNTRY FARMHOUSE WEDDING

Flower Girl Wand

If your wedding venue will not allow your flower girls to toss rose petals, these adorable wands are the perfect substitute! While we created our wands using a color scheme of neutral shades and a mix of materials, you can pick whichever colors and materials work with your wedding theme.

Supply List

Small flat paint brush

Acrylic paint (two contrasting colors)

1 (12-inch long) wood dowel

Distressing brush

Double faced satin ribbon

Sheer ribbon

Lace trim

Sewing machine

Hot glue gun

Silk flower

Scissors

STEP ONE: Using the flat brush and one of your acrylic colors, paint the dowel, and then distress the wood lightly with your distressing brush and the contrasting acrylic color. Allow the paint to dry.

STEP TWO: Cut your satin ribbon, sheer ribbon, and lace into various lengths. You will want three pieces of each material.

STEP THREE: Stack the ribbon and lace strips in one pile and sew one end together using your sewing machine.

STEP FOUR: Place a line of hot glue where the ribbons have been stitched together, and glue the dowel to the ribbons. Roll the ribbon over the dowel and add another line of hot glue near the crease. Roll the dowel again to cover the glue.

STEP FIVE: Place a dot of glue at the top of the dowel and glue the silk flower into place.

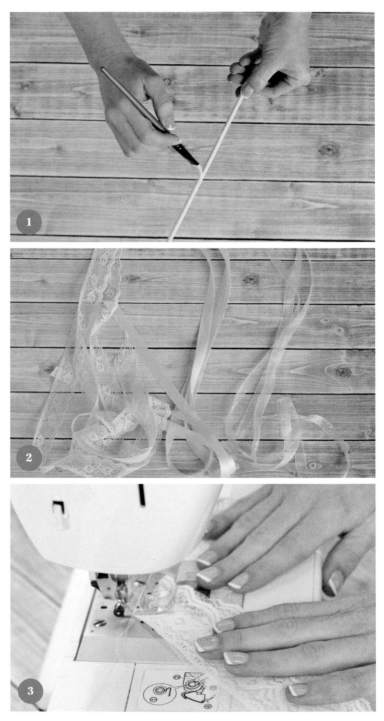

RUSTIC CHIC WEDDING

THE COUNTRY FARMHOUSE WEDDING

Personalized Leather Bouquet Charm

Add a unique personalized touch to *your bridal bouquet with a country chic leather charm. This rustic adornment can be branded with your initials, monogram, or wedding date—a cute keepsake you can repurpose after the wedding.*

Supply List

Pencil

Paper cut-out heart to use as pattern

Crafting leather or suede

Scissors

Leather hole-punch

Multipurpose burning tool/pen

Twine

STEP ONE: Using a pencil, trace your heart pattern onto the crafting leather. Cut the heart out with scissors.

STEP TWO: Using the leather hole-punch, punch a hole in one corner of the heart.

STEP THREE: Pencil your initials or wedding date onto the center of the heart.

STEP FOUR: Using your burning tool, lightly engrave the penciled initials or date into the leather. Thread the twine through the hole in the leather and tie it in a loop.

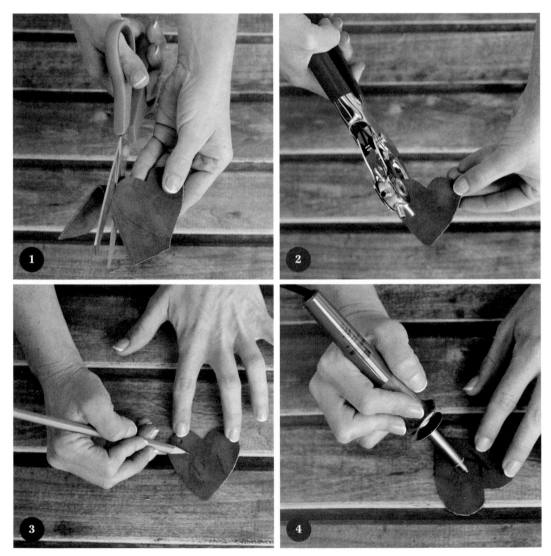

THE COUNTRY FARMHOUSE WEDDING

Pony Garland Necklace

Let your beloved pony—or dog—*join your procession, and adorn her neck with a stunning garland of gorgeous flowers! As your flower girl walks down the aisle, your pet can join her to greet guests and await your arrival.*

Supply List

Muslin fabric

Silk flowers (50 to 100 flowers depending on size of garland)

Hot glue gun

Scissors

STEP ONE: Measure your pony's neck and add an extra 24 inches to this measurement. Cut a 2-inch wide slit into the muslin fabric (to help start the ripping) and rip the length of that total measurement.

STEP TWO: Measure 12 inches from each end of your piece of muslin and tie a knot. Using the hot glue gun, glue your first flower in place on the inside of the knot.

STEP THREE: Add a second flower to the opposite side of the muslin. To completely encircle the muslin, add one or two more flowers and glue them into place.

STEP FOUR: Repeat these steps to completely surround the muslin fabric on all sides with flowers, creating a long garland.

Special Note: To make a garland for a dog, adjust the measurements to comfortably accommodate the dog's neck. A leash can be clipped directly to the muslin knot or to the collar, and hidden under the garland.

Twig Chalkboard "Bride" & "Groom" Chair Signs

Mark your wedding chairs *with these naturally inspired chalkboard signs. Created from twigs and rusty tin wire, they will enhance your country décor and keep with your rustic theme.*

Supply List

Hand drill

2 (8½ x 11-inch) birch wood plaques

Chalkboard paint

Sponge brush

Wire cutters

Bundle of twigs

Rusty tin craft wire

Twine

Scissors

Chalkboard pen

STEP ONE: Drill holes in the top two corners of your birch plaques. Paint your plaques with chalkboard paint using your sponge brush.

STEP TWO: Using the wire cutters, cut half of the twigs into 13-inch lengths and half into 5½-inch lengths. Divide the two lengths into four piles each.

STEP THREE: Wrap each bundle with rusty wire.

STEP FOUR: Connect four bundles (two of each length) together at the corners using the rusty wire.

STEP FIVE: Position your twig frames on top of the chalkboard signs. Drill one hole in the center of each side.

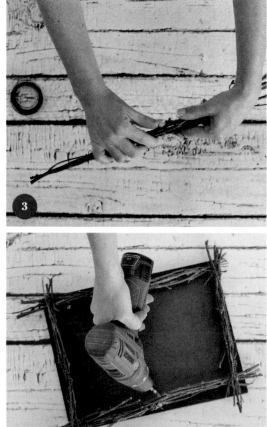

STEP SIX: Feed pieces of rusty wire through the holes in the wood, and connect the twig frame to the chalkboard with your rusty wire by tightly wrapping the wire around the twigs. Use your glue gun to secure any areas that are lifting up.

STEP SEVEN: String the twine through the top two holes in the corner of each board.

STEP EIGHT: Using your chalk pen, elegantly write out "Bride" and "Groom" on the boards.

Special Note
Hang these signs in your kitchen to write grocery lists and little reminder notes!

"Just Married" Sign

This rustic "Just Married" sign can be used in many ways during the wedding. Have your ring bearer carry it down the aisle at the end of the ceremony, use it as a photo prop for pictures, and attach it to your farewell truck as you drive down an old dirt road into the sunset as husband and wife.

Supply List

24 x 5-inch cedar wood plank

Large flat paint brush

Acrylic paint (two contrasting colors)

Distressing paint brush

Grapevine wire

Rusty tin craft wire

Wire cutters

Hammer

Rusty tin craft nails

STEP ONE: Paint the cedar plank with your flat paint brush and one of the acrylic colors, and then distress the edges using the contrasting color and the distressing brush. Allow the paint to dry.

STEP TWO: Twist your grapevine wire to spell out "Just Married." Make one continuous word. The letters should be imperfect and rustic! Use your rusty wire to hold the grapevine wire together.

STEP THREE: Using a few small pieces of grapevine wire, create a separate line to cross the "t" and a heart to dot the "i."

STEP FOUR: Hammer your "Just Married" wire lettering to the wood sign with rusty nails.

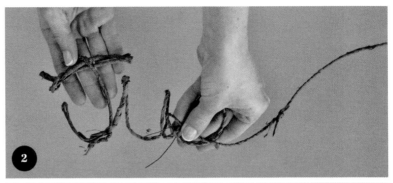

Greet your guests with a handmade guest book that truly represents your personality and style. This handsome country guest book is a wonderful place for your guests to write their well-wishes and advice.

Rustic Guest Book

Supply List

2 (9 x 12-inch) birch wood planks

Sponge brush

Walnut wood stain

Scissors

Craft leather or suede

Pencil

Multipurpose wood burning tool

Leather hole-punch

Hand drill

Antique metal fasteners (copper finish)

25 (8 ½ x 11-inch) sheets cream card stock

Leather suede cord

Hot glue gun

STEP ONE: Stain your birch wood with the sponge brush and walnut stain; allow the wood to dry.

STEP TWO: Using your scissors, cut a 4 x 3-inch rectangle from the craft leather or suede.

STEP THREE: Pencil your names, wedding date, and wedding location onto the piece of leather. Lightly engrave each letter with your burning tool.

STEP FOUR: Using the leather hole-punch, punch a hole into each corner of the leather.

STEP FIVE: Arrange your leather plaque on one of the painted wood planks. Where the punched holes are in the leather, pencil little marks on the wood. Drill holes where your pencil marks are.

(project continues)

THE COUNTRY FARMHOUSE WEDDING

STEP SIX: Attach the leather plaque to the wood with your metal fasteners.

STEP SEVEN: Arrange your card stock paper inside the two wood pieces to make a book. Drill two holes along the left side of the book, and string these holes with pieces of your leather suede cord.

Lucky Horseshoe Table Numbers

These unique table numbers are absolutely perfect for a farmhouse wedding! Full of country charm, they will set the design for each table and add a rustic chic touch to your wedding décor.

Supply List

Old or rusty horseshoes

Cedar wood (several planks, enough to back all of your horseshoes)

Miter saw (not pictured)

Rusty tin craft nails

Wire cutters

Rusty tin craft wire (18 or 22 gauge thickness)

Needle nose pliers

Hammer

Wood burning torch

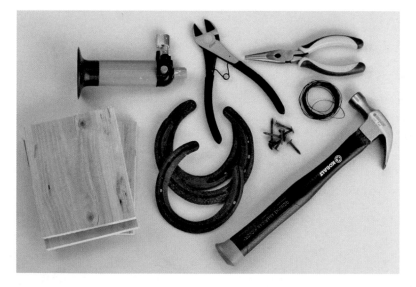

STEP ONE: Measure each of your horseshoes. Have your local hardware store cut your wood to size, or cut the wood yourself using a miter saw.

STEP TWO: Secure a horseshoe to each cedar wood piece using your rusty nails. Before you nail the horseshoe in place, make sure it is nice and centered.

STEP THREE: To make each actual number, you will need to cut four 4 to 8-inch lengths of wire. Keep in mind that your wire length will vary depending on the number you are creating; an "8" will take more wire than a "1".

STEP FOUR: Wrap the four lengths of wire together to make one twisted group; use the needle nose pliers if necessary.

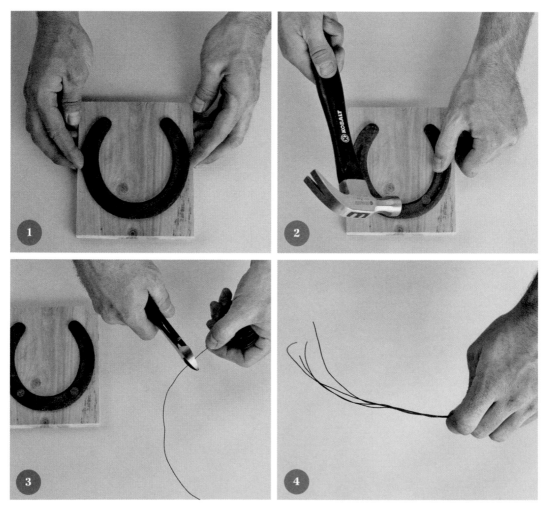

STEP FIVE: Bend the wire into the shape of the number you are creating.

STEP SIX: Curl the ends of each number, as this is where your nails will go through to secure it to the wood.

STEP SEVEN: Hammer the numbers to the wood pieces using the rusty nails. Use as many nails as needed to ensure the number is securely in place.

STEP EIGHT: Scorch the edges of your table numbers with your wood torch to give it a rustic appearance. Make certain to follow the manufactures safety guidelines!

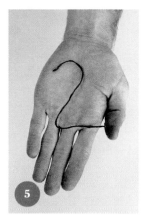

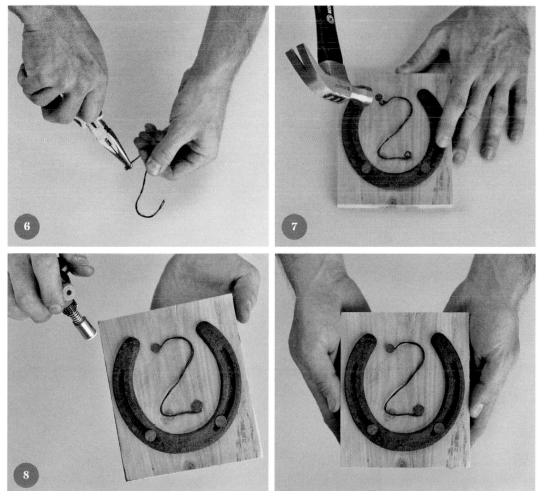

THE COUNTRY FARMHOUSE WEDDING

179

Personalized Placemats

These country chic placemats *have a beautiful love bird theme and double as unique wedding favors your guests can take home!*

STEP ONE: Cut your burlap fabric into 16 x 12-inch placemats.

STEP TWO: Cut your muslin into 4 x 2-inch patches.

STEP THREE: Stamp each muslin patch with a guest's name along a tree branch and a love bird.

STEP FOUR: Using the needle and floss, sew a stamped muslin patch onto each burlap placemat using long straight stitches.

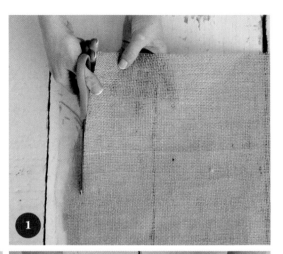

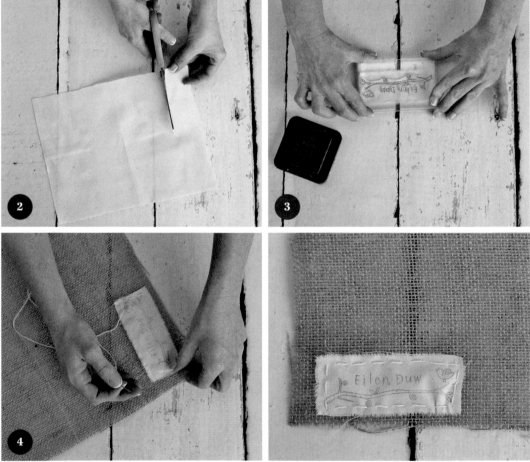

"Mr. & Mrs." Shot Glass Holders

These rustic shot glass holders are the *perfect accessory for your country wedding. The unique design is both hilarious and cute and will make your wedding photos truly remarkable.*

Special Note: This project is for advanced crafters. Be extremely careful when using the tools needed to create this design—follow all safety precautions, and protect your eyes, limbs, and fingers.

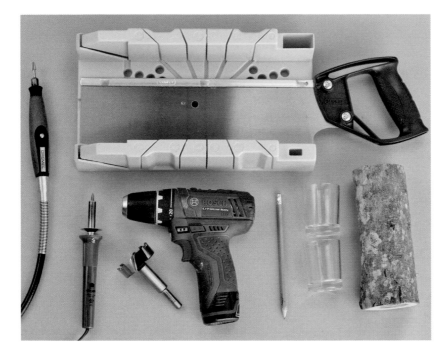

Supply List

8-inch maple or birch
wood log (at least 2 ½
inches in diameter)

Miter saw or hand saw

Hand drill or drill press

2-inch drill bit (or
larger to accommodate
your shot glass)

Pencil

Rotary tool (dremel)

Carving bit

Multipurpose wood
burning tool/pen

2 shot glasses

STEP ONE: Cut the log in half using your saw.

STEP TWO: Using your drill and 2-inch drill bit, bore a hole about 1 inch deep in the top of each log. Make sure to use a slow drill speed.

STEP THREE: Trace a heart on the front of each log piece. Using your rotary tool with the carving bit, slowly engrave the heart shape. Take your time; patience will ensure that your hearts look clean and nice.

(project continues)

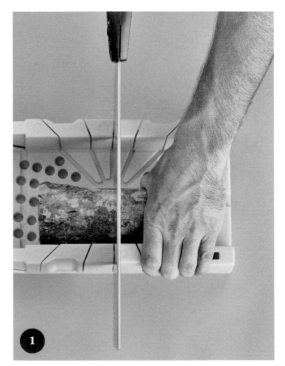

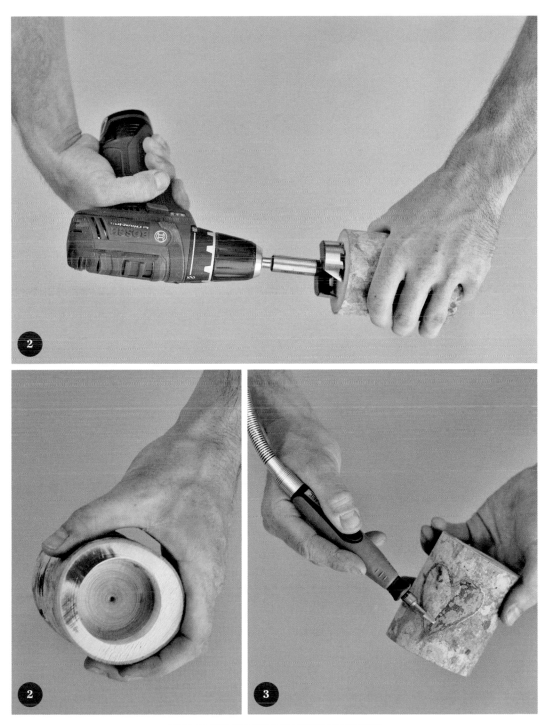

STEP FOUR: With your multipurpose burning tool, engrave "Mr." and "Mrs." into the heart. Sketch it first if you need to, and remember to go slowly. Place your shot glasses in holder logs. Drink up!

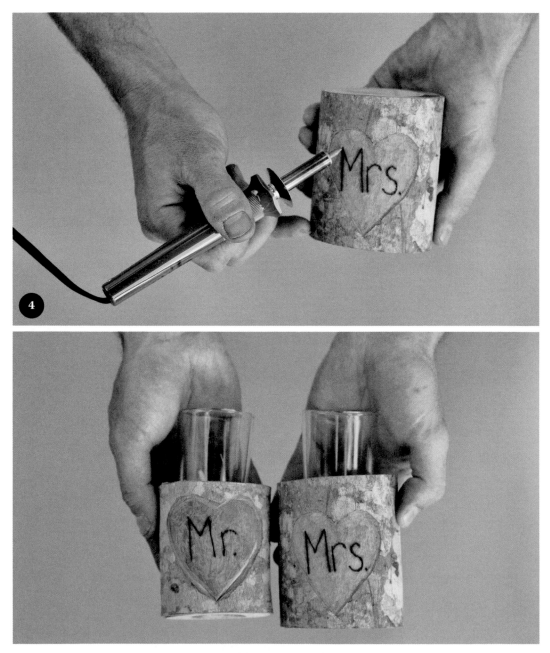

Lighted Bar Sign

Lead the way to your reception bar with this bright sign; your wedding guests will certainly get a kick out of it!

Flat paint brush

1 (12 x 5-inch) cedar wood plank

Acrylic paint in contrasting colors (brown and yellow)

Distressing paint brush

Round lettering brush

Battery operated lights (and batteries)

Hand drill

Brown duct tape

STEP ONE: Using the flat brush, paint the cedar plank with brown acrylic paint, and then distress it with yellow paint using the distressing brush. Allow the paint to dry.

STEP TWO: Using your yellow paint and the lettering brush, paint "BAR" onto your sign; rustic letters are just fine!

THE COUNTRY FARMHOUSE WEDDING

STEP THREE: Count the number of lights on your string of lights. Drill this quantity of holes along the letters in your sign.

STEP FOUR: Place your lights inside the holes. Use the brown duct tape to secure the lights into place on the back of the sign. Tape the battery pack so that the on/off switch is accessible.

This picturesque cake stand matches perfectly with the twig cake topper (page 194); it is so versatile and will complement nearly any wedding cake!

Twig Cake Stand

Supply List

Simple wood cake stand

Clear drying wood glue

Small twig sticks (enough to border your entire cake stand)

1-inch paint brush

Mixing jar

STEP ONE: Set the cake stand up on one edge. Using your wood glue, run a ¼-inch bead across the center of the top edge.

STEP TWO: Press the sticks into the glue, arranging them so they are flush with the base of the cake stand. Let the glue dry for 2 hours or completely dry.

STEP THREE: In the mixing jar, dilute more of the wood glue with water in a 3-to-1 ratio and brush it over the sticks. Use sparingly and allow the glue to dry completely. Repeat these steps on the three remaining sides of the cake stand.

THE COUNTRY FARMHOUSE WEDDING

Twig Cake Topper

This primitive cake topper will add a personalized rustic touch to your wedding cake.

Special Note: Your initials will most likely be different than the initials we are creating; therefore, you will need to alter the directions slightly to suit your needs.

Supply List

6 brown paper–covered stem wires (each 12 inches long)

25 pieces grapevine (each 12 inches long)

Rusty tin craft wire

Wire cutters

Needle nose pliers

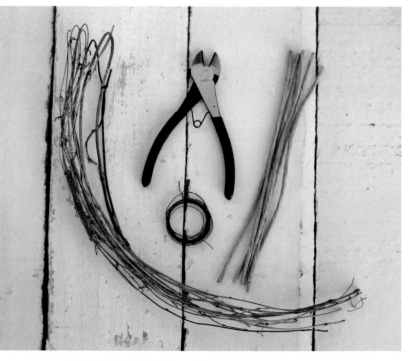

RUSTIC CHIC WEDDING

THE COUNTRY FARMHOUSE WEDDING

STEP ONE: Twist your brown paper–covered stem wires to form a heart and each of your initials: each initial should be about 5 inches tall with one long piece that will hold it in place on the cake. Use small pieces of the craft wire to hold more than one piece together if needed.

STEP TWO: Cut the grapevines into 5-inch segments, and then divide the grapevine into piles of 5 segments each. You'll need one stack for each part of the letter: for instance, a "K" would need three bundles of grapevine, and an "M" would need four. Cut the rusty wire into 5 inch pieces, and twist each grapevine stack nice and tight with three pieces of rusty wire, using needle nose pliers if necessary.

STEP THREE: Attach the grapevine bundles to your wire letters with more rusty wire.

CHAPTER FIVE

The Classics

In this chapter you will find some of our most popular designs. With step-by-step directions, we have made it easier than ever to make a love bird cake topper, vow books, personalized firefly lanterns, and more!

Firefly Lantern

One of our most cherished designs, these firefly lanterns are reminiscent of sweet childhood memories—running through pastures at twilight and catching fireflies. Hang these lanterns along your wedding aisle, suspend them from trees, or place one at each table for unique lighting. They will certainly make a magical statement.

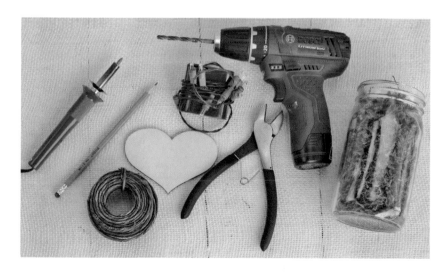

Supply List

Pencil

4-inch wide wood heart

Hand drill

Multipurpose wood burning tool/pen

Grapevine wire (24 to 36 inches long, depending on your jar)

Wide mouth glass jars

Preserved moss

Battery operated lights (and batteries)

STEP ONE: Pencil your initials onto your wood heart.

STEP TWO: Drill holes in both sides of the heart.

STEP THREE: Using your multipurpose burning tool, engrave your initials into the wood.

STEP FOUR: Twist your grapevine wire into a circle just larger than the jar's opening. Make sure you have one short end and one long end.

STEP FIVE: Push the circle against the jar and bend half the circle up to make your handle. Wrap the long end around the mouth of the jar to secure the handle. You should now have two short ends sticking out from the jar.

STEP SIX: Run the two ends of grapevine wire through the holes in your wood heart and twist the grapevines around the jar to secure the heart.

STEP SEVEN: Pack the moss and lights inside the jar.

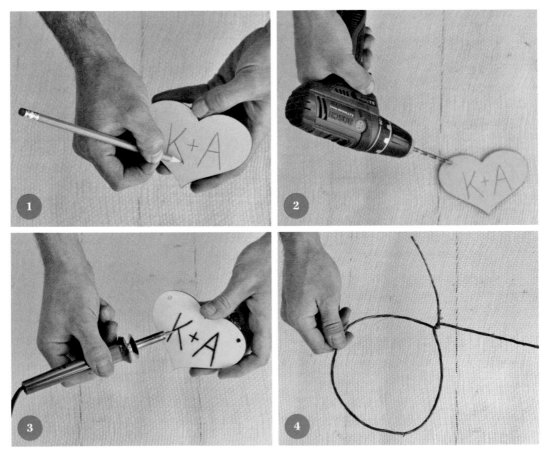

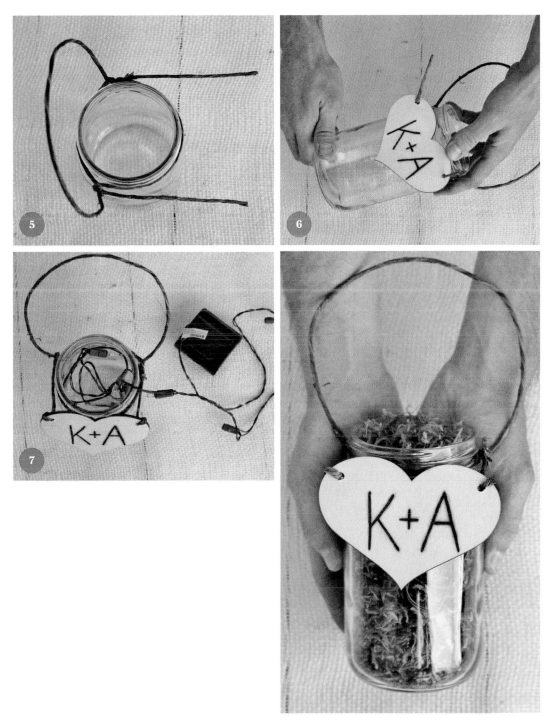

Vow
Books

These amazing little books *will forever hold your words of commitment and affirmation; let them be loved for a lifetime and passed down to your children and grandchildren as mementos of your love story.*

Supply List

Vow book template
(page 263)

2 (4 x 3-inch) faux
wood paper
mâché books

Pencil

Scissors

Graphite transfer
paper

Multipurpose
burning tool/pen

Distressing brush

Acrylic paint
in cream

STEP ONE: Print two copies of the vow book template on regular paper and cut them out with your scissors.

STEP TWO: Cut a piece of graphite paper to fit between each book and template. Once everything is lined up perfectly, use your pencil to trace the design onto the books. Remove the template and graphite paper.

STEP THREE: Pencil your initials into heart on each book cover. If you would rather use the lettering template (page 262), scan the template and resize the letters to fit inside the hearts. Print the letters, cut them out, and transfer them to the books using the directions in Step Two.

STEP FOUR: Lightly go over the transfer with your multipurpose burning tool to engrave the design.

STEP FIVE: Using your distressing brush and the cream acrylic paint, very lightly go over the book to give it a rustic finish.

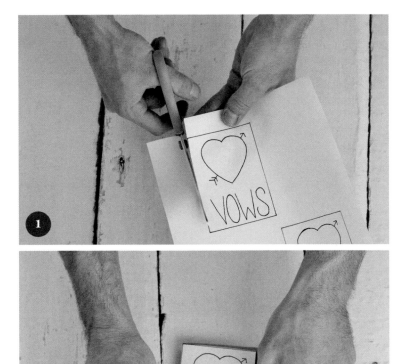

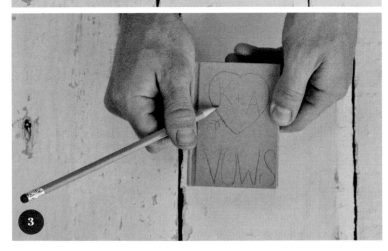

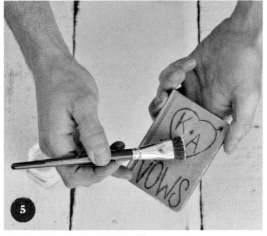

Special Note:
While I have hand-engraved these books, you can easily skip this step and use a dark brown paint pen over your pencil markings! The finished design will be just as lovely.

Love Bird Cake Topper

Our love bird cake toppers *will add an adorable finishing touch to your wedding cake. They are so versatile that they complement nearly any theme including rustic, woodland, farmhouse, vintage chic, garden, flea market—you name it!*

Special Note: While I have hand-engraved these love birds, you can easily skip this step and use a dark brown paint pen over your pencil markings. You can also switch out the wood birds for card stock paper cut-outs if you prefer.

Supply List

Love bird cake topper templates (page 264 and 265)

Scissors

2 (4-inch) wood love bird cutouts

Graphite transfer paper

Pencil

Multipurpose burning tool/pen

Hot glue gun

2 wood dowels (each inches long)

Cream or off-white felt

STEP ONE: Copy the templates onto regular paper and cut them out with scissors.

STEP TWO: Using the wood love birds as guides, trace the outline of each bird onto a piece of graphite paper and cut them out.

STEP THREE: Place your graphite paper love birds in between your wood love birds and your templates. Once everything is lined up perfectly, trace the letters with your pencil to transfer them to the wood birds. Remove the templates and graphite paper.

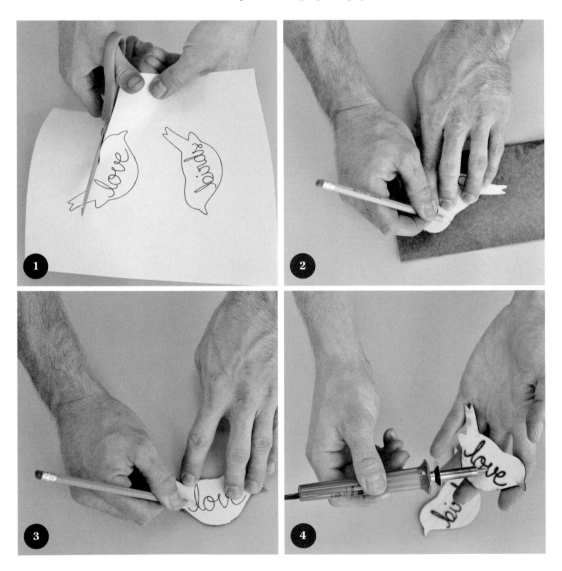

STEP FOUR: Go over the transfers with your multipurpose burning tool to burn the letters into the wood.

STEP FIVE: Lightly burn the edges of your love birds with the side of your engraving tool.

STEP SIX: Glue your wood dowels to the back of your love birds, using the hot glue gun.

STEP SEVEN: Cut two 1-inch felt circles. Glue one to the back of each love bird to hide the place where you attached the wood dowels.

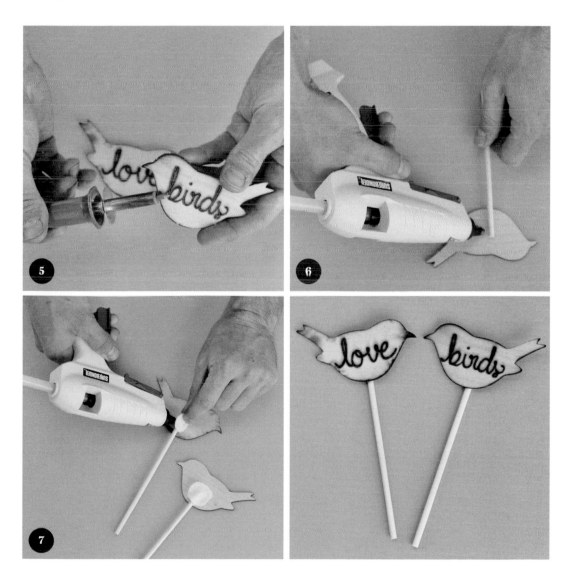

Ring Security Box

One of our newest designs, *this is a clever alternative to the traditional ring bearer pillow. You will surely see a ton of smiles from your guests as your ring bearer walks down the aisle.*

Supply List

Medium flat paint brush

Acrylic paint (two contrasting colors)

Wood or paper mâché box, about 6 to 8 inches wide

Distressing brush

Pencil

Small lettering brush

Two small wood circles (one larger than the other)

Hot glue gun

Burlap fabric

Chenille needle

Cotton six-strand floss in cream

Pillow stuffing

Twine

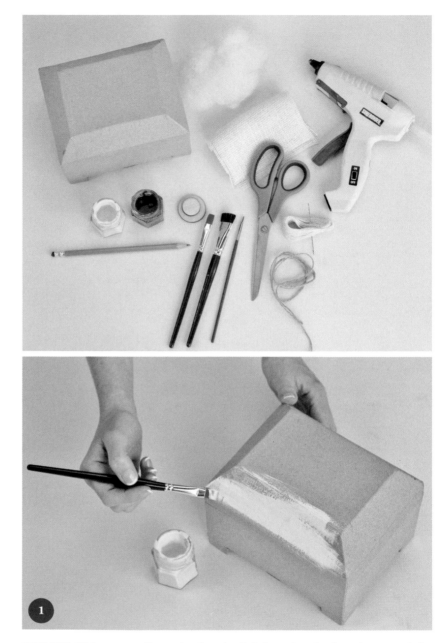

STEP ONE: Using your flat paint brush, lightly paint the box in one of the acrylic colors. Gently dab your distressing brush into your contrasting paint color and go over the edges of the box to give it a worn appearance. Allow the paint to dry.

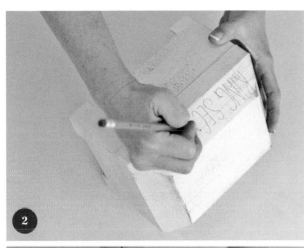

STEP TWO: Using your pencil, write out "RING SECURITY" on the top of the box.

STEP THREE: Using the lettering brush, paint over the letters with your contrasting acrylic color. Allow the paint to dry.

STEP FOUR: Using the flat brush, paint the round wood circles with your contrasting color. Allow the paint to dry. Glue the smaller circle onto the larger circle with your hot glue gun. On the larger circle, add lines to mimic a dial.

(project continues)

THE CLASSICS

STEP FIVE: Measure the center of your box and glue the fake dial to the front.

STEP SIX: Measure the inside of your box and cut two pieces of burlap to accommodate this size.

STEP SEVEN: Place your two pieces of burlap on top of each other. Using the needle and floss, begin sewing with large straight stitches, leaving a ½-inch edge and a 3-inch opening to allow for stuffing.

STEP EIGHT: Add stuffing to the inside of the pillow. Smooth the stuffing so that it is evenly dispersed inside the pillow.

STEP NINE: Sew the remaining area of the pillow so it is now complete. Cut the edges of the pillow so they look balanced. Wrap the twine around the pillow and tie it into a bow. Attach your rings to this twine.

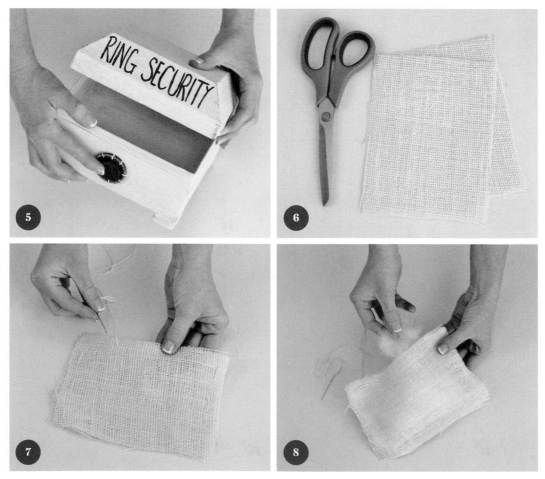

Grapevine Ball Lanterns

Hanging from old willow trees, these grapevine lanterns add an allure of enchantment and beauty! The flickering lights will give a warm glow to your dusk ceremony and evening reception. To save time, you can purchase pre-made grapevine balls instead of making your own.

Supply List

Rusty tin craft wire

Wire cutters

Grapevine garland

Balloons (1 per lantern)

Moss or faux rose petals

Battery operated lights (and batteries)

Special Note: After the wedding, hang these lanterns in a tight cluster above your dining room table as a beautiful rustic chandelier.

STEP ONE: Cut the rusty wire into fifty 3-inch strips.

STEP TWO: Unroll the grapevines and cut them into thin pieces, 16 to 24 inches long. Overlap the ends of the pieces and tie them with the 3-inch strips of wire to make one long continuous piece of grapevine. This long piece should measure about 15 feet long to make a smaller lantern. To make a larger lantern, create a longer continuous grapevine.

STEP THREE: Blow up one of the balloons. Place the beginning of the grapevine through the knot of the balloon to hold it in place. Very carefully begin wrapping the long strand of grapevine completely around the balloon, layer over layer over layer.

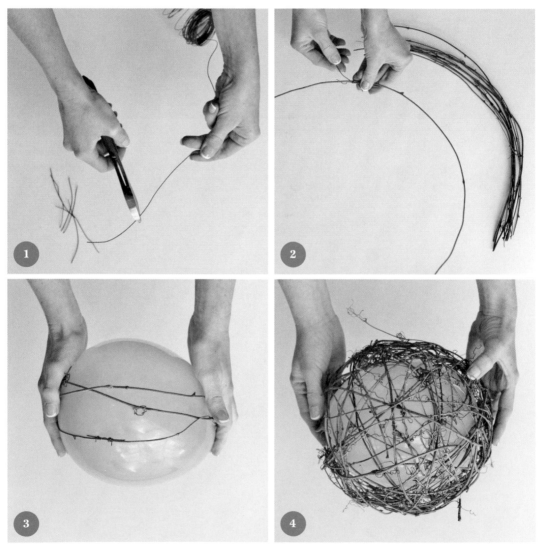

STEP FOUR: When the balloon is completely wrapped in grapevine, pop the balloon and remove it.

STEP FIVE: Add moss to the inside of the grape-vine ball. Turn on the lights and carefully slip them inside of the grapevine ball; hide the battery pack inside the moss. Arrange the grapevines to close the ball completely.

STEP SIX: To make a handle, attach a short piece of grapevine to the top of the lantern, securing it with wire.

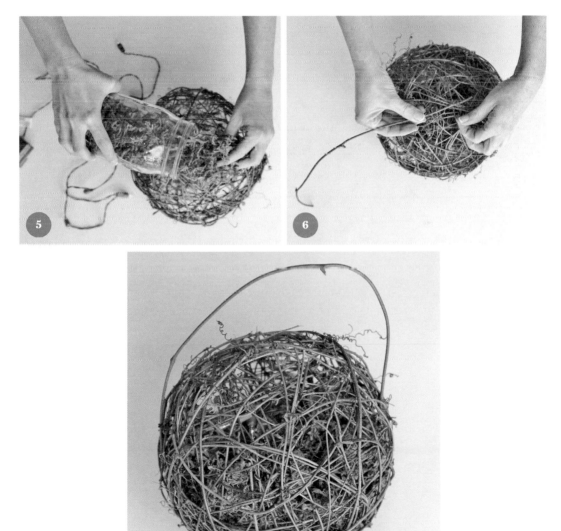

CHAPTER SIX

Bridal Bouquets & Bout Pins

Your wedding flowers should showcase your personality, style, and character. What you hold in your hands as you walk down the aisle to marry your true love symbolizes your emotions and individuality.

In this chapter we will step away from the traditional and add uniqueness and glamour to your bouquet. Using only the finest silk flowers, you can create amazing bridal bouquets for you and your whole party!

The Rustic Bouquet

Supply List

Wire cutters

5 white silk anemones

8 white silk carnations

8 white silk ranunculus

5 white silk roses

3 dried Lotus pods

10 dried foxtails (save two foxtails for the bout pin)

Filler sprigs of cream wax flowers (save two sprigs for the bout pin)

White floral tape

Cream double faced satin ribbon

Vintage lace doily

Cream sheer ribbon

STEP ONE: Using wire cutters, remove the leaves from your silk flower stems.

STEP TWO: Cut your stems so they are about 12 inches long.

STEP THREE: Start with an anemone and then add a carnation, a ranunculus, and a rose. Add one flower at a time to the bunch, keeping it well balanced. Do not add the lotus pods, foxtails, or fillers yet.

STEP FOUR: Fluff each flower as you go and open its petals; guide the wire stems so the flowers are at a pleasing angle. Carefully continue to add your flowers to your bouquet, positioning the flowers so the different species are spread throughout the arrangement and not clumped into one area.

STEP FIVE: When your bouquet is nice and full, you can then add your lotus pods, foxtails, and fillers by pushing them down into the bouquet. Your finished bouquet will be about 8 inches in diameter.

STEP SIX: Wrap the middle of the stems with white floral tape to secure the bouquet. Cut any stems that are too long.

(project continues)

STEP SEVEN: Place a dot of hot glue on one end of the satin ribbon, and wrap the ribbon around the floral tape. Secure the ribbon at the top of the stems with another dot of glue.

STEP EIGHT: Wrap the doily around your stems and tie a piece of sheer ribbon at the top to secure it.

The Bout Pin

STEP ONE: Cut the reserved dried foxtails and filler sprigs so they measure 4 inches long.

STEP TWO: Hold the stems together and wrap them with floral tape.

STEP THREE: Wrap the satin ribbon around the floral tape and secure the ribbon with a dot of hot glue; turn the edges of the ribbon in to hide the end cuts.

The Vintage Shabby
Couture Bridal Bouquet

Supply List

Wire cutters

8 large silk Eden roses (mix of pink, cream, and white)

8 pink silk ranunculus

7 cream and white silk roses (save one rose for the bout pin)

10 silk blooming peonies and buds (mix of pink, cream, and white)

White floral tape

Pale pink double faced satin ribbon

Pale pink sheer ribbon

Rhinestone button (new or old)

Filler flowers for bout pin

Wood twists for bout pin

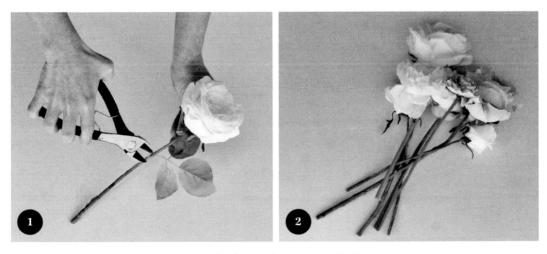

STEP ONE: Using wire cutters, remove the leaves from your silk flower stems.

STEP TWO: Cut your stems so they are about 13 inches long.

STEP THREE: Begin with your largest Eden rose and then add a few ranunculus, roses, and peonies.

STEP FOUR: Continually fluff and rearrange the flowers so that the bouquet is balanced and has a nice circular design. Continue adding more roses and ranunculus. Separate the larger Eden roses and peonies throughout the bouquet and bend the wire stems to fill in any gaps or holes in the arrangement.

STEP FIVE: When your design is round and full, pull a few of the ranunculus out just slightly to add a bit of depth to the bouquet. Your finished bouquet will be about 14 inches in diameter.

STEP SIX: Wrap the middle of the stems in your white floral tape to secure the bouquet. If any of your stems are extra long, trim them.

(project continues)

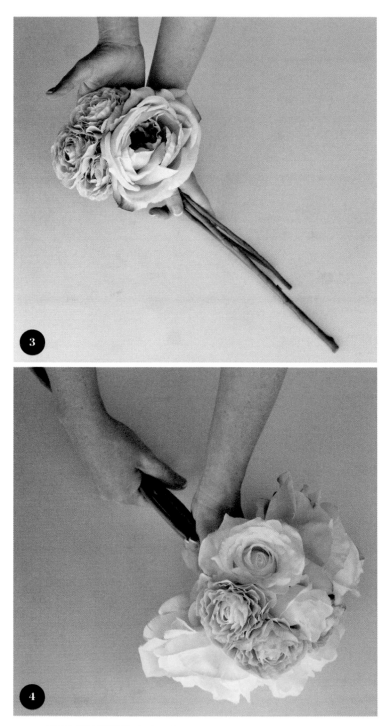

RUSTIC CHIC WEDDING

THE BRIDAL BOUQUET AND BOUT PIN

STEP SEVEN: Place a dot of hot glue on one end of the satin ribbon, and wrap the ribbon around the floral tape. Secure the ribbon at the top of the stems with another dot of glue.

STEP EIGHT: Use your sheer pink ribbon to attach your rhinestone button to the base of the bouquet.

The Bout Pin

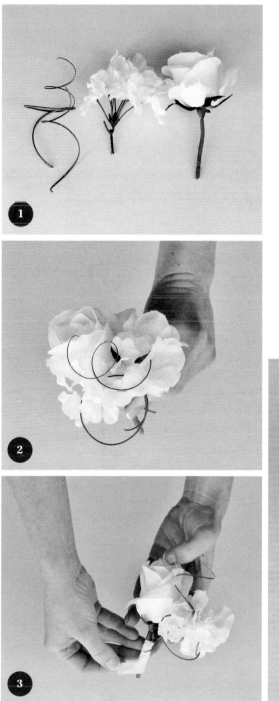

STEP ONE: Cut your rose, filler flowers, and wood twits so they measure 4 inches long.

STEP TWO: Position your rose, filler flowers, and wood twits together. Wrap the stems in floral tape.

STEP THREE: Wrap double faced satin ribbon around the floral tape and secure it with a dot of hot glue; turn the edges of the ribbon in to hide the end cuts.

The Fall Harvest Bouquet

Supply List

Wire cutters

5 silk sunflowers

5 purple silk hyacinths

7 deep purple silk hydrangeas

3 yellow silk blooming roses

19 mini silk daisies (save 3 for the bout pin)

9 silk billy buttons (save two for the bout pin)

5 silk tweedia flower sprigs (save one spring for the bout pin)

White floral tape

Scissors

White double faced satin ribbon

White lace trim

STEP ONE: Using wire cutters, remove the leaves from your silk flower stems and put one leaf aside for your bout pin.

STEP TWO: Cut your stems so they are about 14 inches long.

STEP THREE: Begin with your largest sunflower and then add a few hyacinths, hydrangeas, and roses.

STEP FOUR: Bend the wires of each stem so the flowers are pointing in different directions.

STEP FIVE: When your design is circular and lavish, add a few billy buttons, daisies, and your tweedia flower sprigs by pushing them into place. The design of your bouquet should be untamed and natural looking, with the flowers cascading and arranged at different heights throughout. Your finished bouquet will be about 14 inches in diameter.

STEP SIX: Wrap the middle of the stems in white floral tape to secure the bouquet. If any of your stems are extra long, trim them.

STEP SEVEN: Place a dot of hot glue on one end of the satin ribbon, and wrap the ribbon around the floral tape. Secure the ribbon at the top of the stems with another dot of glue.

STEP EIGHT: Cut a piece of lace about 20 inches long. Using your glue gun, add a line of glue along the edge of the lace and secure it to the stems. Wrap the lace over the ribbon and glue the loose end down.

THE BRIDAL BOUQUET AND BOUT PIN

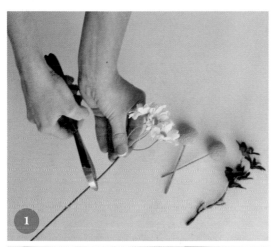

The Bout Pin

STEP ONE: Cut your daisies, tweedia flower sprig, and billy buttons so they measure 4 inches long. Put your reserved leaf aside.

STEP TWO: Layer your billy buttons, mini daisies, and tweedia sprig by height. Wrap the stems in floral tape and glue your leaf to the back.

STEP THREE: Wrap double faced satin ribbon around the floral tape and secure it with a dot of glue; turn the edges of the ribbon in to hide the end cuts.

The Garden Fresh Bouquet

Supply List

Wire cutters

12 silk roses, a mix of pink, cream, and white (save one blooming rose and one bud for the bout pin)

14 blooming peonies and buds, a mix of pink, cream, and white

12 ranunculus, a mix of pink, cream, and white

White floral tape

Scissors

Cream double faced satin ribbon

Lace trim (a cut from your mother's wedding dress or new lace will do)

Wood twist (for your bout pin)

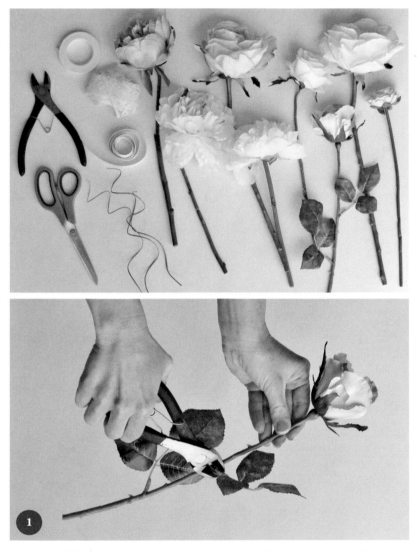

STEP ONE: Using your wire cutters, remove any leaves from the silk flower stems. Place one leaf aside for your bout pin.

STEP TWO: Cut your stems so they are about 14 inches long.

STEP THREE: Group together a few of your roses and blooming peonies. Arrange them in a round design and then continue to add your remaining flowers to the perimeter, one by one. Your finished bouquet will be about 12 inches in diameter.

STEP FOUR: When your bouquet is thick, full, and round, wrap the stems with floral tape. Fluff the flowers to enlarge their shape and soften their blooms.

STEP FIVE: Place a dot of hot glue on one end of the satin ribbon, and wrap the ribbon around the floral tape. Secure the ribbon at the top of the stems with another dot of glue.

STEP SIX: Cut a piece of lace about 20 inches long. Using your glue gun, add a line of glue along the edge of the lace and secure it to the stems. Wrap the lace over the ribbon and glue the loose end down.

The Bout Pin

STEP ONE: Cut your rose stem and wood twist to measure 4 inches long.

STEP TWO: Arrange your blooming rose and bud side by side. Place your wood twist on top of the roses. Wrap the stems in floral tape.

STEP THREE: Glue your leaves to the back of the bout pin. Wrap double-faced satin ribbon around the floral tape and secure it with a dot of hot glue; turn the edges of the ribbon in to hide the end cuts.

STEP FOUR: Cut a piece of lace about 6 inches long. Using your glue gun, add a line of glue along the edge of the lace and secure it to the stems. Wrap the lace over the ribbon and glue the loose end down.

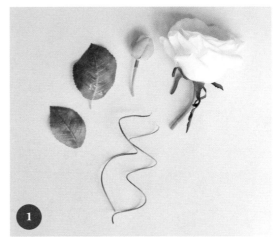

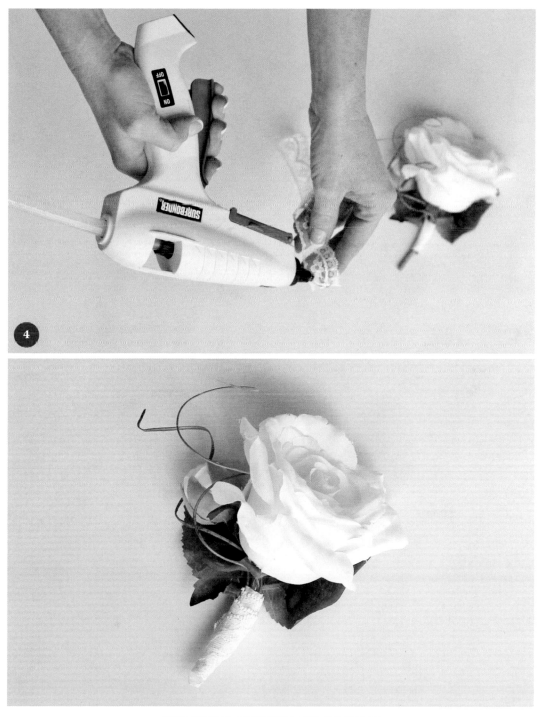

THE BRIDAL BOUQUET AND BOUT PIN

The Purely Elegant Bouquet

Supply List

Wire cutters

13 white silk cabbage roses

16 blooming silk ranunculus, a mix of deep purples and white (save two blooms for the bout pin)

12 purple mini silk ranunculus

6 bunches silk hydrangeas

8 purple silk anemones

White floral tape

Scissors

White satin double faced ribbon

Cream lace trim

Large vintage brooch

STEP ONE: Using your wire cutters, remove any leaves from the silk flower stems. Save two leaves for your bout pin.

STEP TWO: Cut your stems so they are 14 inches long.

STEP THREE: Arrange your cabbage roses and blooming ranunculus into a small bunch. Continue to add more roses, hydrangeas, and the mini ranunculus. Balance the colors by spreading them throughout the bouquet.

STEP FOUR: When your arrangement is abundant, pull gently on the blooms to fluff them. Adjust a few ranunculuses so they are slightly taller for depth. Your finished bouquet will be about 14 inches in diameter.

STEP FIVE: Wrap your stems in your floral tape. Place a dot of hot glue on one end of the satin ribbon, and wrap the ribbon around the floral tape. Secure the ribbon at the top of the stems with another dot of glue.

STEP SIX: Cut a piece of lace about 20 inches long. Using your glue gun, add a line of glue along the edge of the lace and secure it to the stems. Wrap the lace over the ribbon and glue the loose end down. Attach your large vintage brooch to the lace.

RUSTIC CHIC WEDDING

THE BRIDAL BOUQUET AND BOUT PIN

The Bout Pin

STEP ONE: Cut your ranunculus to measure 4 inches long.

STEP TWO: Arrange the two ranunculus side by side and place your two leaves behind them. Wrap the stems in floral tape.

STEP THREE: Cover the floral tape with white double faced satin ribbon, securing the ribbon with a dot of hot glue. Turn the edges of the ribbon in to hide the end cuts. Cut a piece of lace about 6 inches long. Using your glue gun, add a line of glue along the edge of the lace and secure it to the stems. Wrap the lace over the ribbon and glue the loose end down.

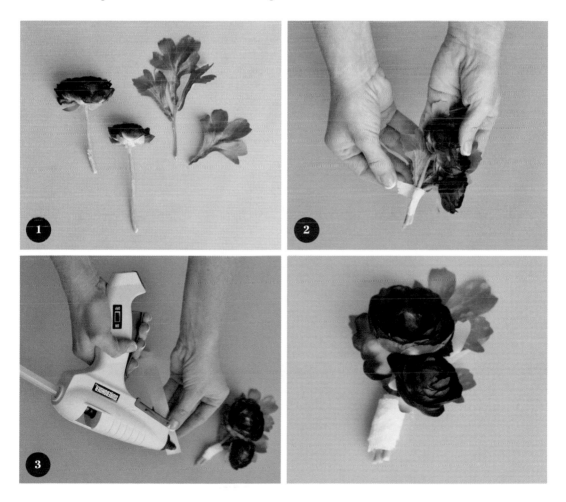

CHAPTER SEVEN

Deconstructed Tablescapes

In this chapter we will deconstruct three uniquely crafted wedding tablescapes and discuss the specific elements that bring each table design together. This section is full of inspiration and ideas that you can adjust to accommodate your unique theme.

Pick Your Flower Seating Chart

Invite your guests to sit anywhere they would like with this creative seating chart! Set up a long table with jars filled with fresh flowers in an array of blooms.

1. THE WELCOME BANNER: Create a large banner to welcome your guests and guide them to your decorative flower seating chart. Using a few large wood hearts and a burning tool, burn your message onto the hearts and string them together to create a rustic chic banner.

2. THE WELCOME SIGN: Create a rustic wood sign to welcome your guests and give them clear instructions on picking their own seat! The ladies can place their flowers in their hair as a colorful accessory, and the men can place their flowers in their buttonholes.

3. THE FLOWER JARS: Count the number of seats you will have available per table. Add that quantity of flowers to each jar, allowing guests to pick a flower and choose the table where they would like to sit. This creative gesture will bring your guests together in an entertaining fashion. Mark each jar by engraving the table number and type of flower onto a sweet little wood heart to complement your welcome banner.

Fun Idea! Keep the theme alive and decorate each table with its coordinating flower! For example, Table One will have a centerpiece full of pink roses; Table Two will have a centerpiece full of yellow carnations, and so on.

4. THE SIGNAGE: This nostalgic sign is a great way to point your guests in the right direction! Label the different arrows and arrange them in the appropriate directions.

5. TABLE DECORATIONS: You can accessorize your table with rustic candles, primitive décor, and old linens.

6. THE FLOWER CART: Place an old flower cart in front of your welcome table and fill it with fresh flowers. We used tall antique mason jars and filled them with an array of different blooms in bright colors.

The Kids' Table

Every wedding should have a designated "kid friendly" area. A great wedding is all about mingling, dancing, and enjoying the company of others—regardless of age. The children at your wedding will be absolutely giddy when they see the special table you have designed just for their enjoyment! A well thought out kids' table will also give parents a chance to relax as their little ones play happily.

1. THE TABLE: We used an old rustic coffee table as our kids' table; since the table is low to the ground it can easily and safely accommodate children. Create an inexpensive table cover with a few yards of muslin fabric, and tie the edges around the legs of the table so the tablecloth stays in place. Mix and match old kid chairs and place them around the table.

2. "KIDS ONLY" SIGN: Using a piece of old rustic wood, paint a cute "Kids Only" sign and place it on the table.

3. SWEET TREATS & PERSONALIZED SEATS: Decorate your table top with an array of sweet treats. On a tree-slice stand, pile kid-friendly candy and desserts. Use paper doilies to accent each delicious treat, and spell out the first initial of each of your little guests' names using mini old-fashioned candy sticks. Fill mason jars with rock candy and shiny gumballs, and tie your napkins with red vines.

4. EVERY ACCESSORY COUNTS: Decorate the table with glass-handled mason jars filled with juice, and place fun, colorful straws in each jar. Using drilled maple logs (like the project on page 183), place crayons at each place setting for the kids to doodle and draw.

The Extra Extraordinary Candy Bar

Tempt your wedding guests with a table full of mouth watering sweets and desserts! A few hours before the final farewell, let your guests graze on an impressive selection of cake, candy, doughnuts, and pastries.

1. **THE LAYOUT:** Arrange your sweets on a long slender table at various heights. Use cake stands to elevate your desserts, and convert old frames into trays to showcase your delightful treats. You can also use apothecary jars in various sizes to add depth and dimension to your layout. We placed a pretty pink chair next to our dessert table and covered our tables with pretty linens.

2. THE CAKE: You can accent a plain cake using pretty and inexpensive candy. It would usually cost hundreds of dollars for a baker to roll fondant balls, but it cost us only a few dollars to accent our cake with these affordable gumballs!

3. THE DOUGHNUT DISPLAY: We crafted a clever doughnut display and made that our main focal point of the table. Pick a color palette of beautiful shades that complement your other wedding décor, and order (or make) your desserts to match your theme.

4. CHALKBOARD MARKERS: Use little chalkboard signs to mark each dessert accordingly. (You can make them yourself using the project on page 125!)

5. FRESH FLOWERS: To add another layer of exquisiteness to your table, place roses in little bud vases and scatter them around the table. Place fresh flowers on top of cakes and mini desserts for color and added beauty.

Templates

A B C D E

F G H I J K

L M N O P

Q R S T U

V W X Y Z

a b c d e f g h i

j k l m n o p q r

s t u v w x y z

1 2 3 4 5 6 7

8 9 0 & . , ! ?

Bride

Groom

Acknowledgments

To my parents Phil & Eileen, thank you for always believing in me and my art. To Rocky & Margie, thank you for Kyle and Arkansas.

To all the brides and grooms that have purchased my creations over the years—the biggest thank you. It is because of you that this book is a reality; I am humble and thankful for your support. And to you, the reader, believe in yourself and your ability to create. Let this book help guide you as you make beautiful art for your wedding that in the coming years you will look back on and remember with a smile. Thank you from the bottom of my heart.

Queen of Cakes & Café (queenofcakesandcafe.com): Thank you so much for your contributions; the cakes were amazing!

Archive Rentals (archiverentals.com): Thank you for all the amazing antique rentals. Your furniture and accessories are breathtaking!

Lauren Sharon Vintage Shop Rentals (vintagerentalssandiego.com). Thank you for supplying beautiful pieces of rustic furniture and decor.

Thank you to Stephanie & Brandon, Janel & Jolie, Tiffany & Corbin, Heather & Pete, Maddie, Ashley, Emily, Luci, Mugga & Boppa, and everyone who tirelessly helped make this book a reality. I am forever grateful for your support.

Index